MATCH SHORE FISHING

An example of the over-crowding problem when fishing in some pier matches.

MATCH
SHORE
FISHING

Bob Gledhill

ADAM & CHARLES BLACK · LONDON

FIRST PUBLISHED 1972
BY A. AND C. BLACK LIMITED
4, 5 AND 6 SOHO SQUARE LONDON W1V 6AD

© 1972 BOB GLEDHILL

ISBN 0 7136 1333 5

DEDICATION

*To the
Lady Anglers of Redcar*

PRINTED BY
REDWOOD PRESS LIMITED, TROWBRIDGE, WILTSHIRE

Contents

Illustrations

I know of very few anglers who don't take some form of delight in winning sea fishing matches. Even those who profess to be real 'loners' must feel a glow of pride when their name is announced as the winner. But it's apparent that on the shoreline there are anglers whose names seem to crop up with a regularity that you can't dismiss as pure luck.

The fact is that on the day of the match they had something that every other angler hadn't. It might have been preparation; the angler who goes into a fishing tackle shop on a Saturday afternoon and buys what bait is going, turns up with a tackle box looking like the Amazon jungle and sits down on the beach just anywhere, can't expect to win. There are certainly cases when this does happen but they are so rare that when they do they make headline news.

We have all heard stories of the angler who enters a contest on the spur of the moment. He goes down to the water—usually late—makes a bad cast that lands a few feet out and catches a fish that wins the match. However, relying on that kind of luck is having too much faith in providence.

It is also true to say that the sea angler who can catch fish in a match can do the same in pleasure fishing. There is not this dividing line in sea fishing that exists in freshwater between the matchman and the specimen hunter. If you can learn to take fish quickly and in quantity during a match you will also learn how to take specimen fish at other times.

The days when you could go down to the beach and 'try your luck' are fast disappearing. It is the age of the specialists, who are prepared to put extra effort in to get an extra return. With prizes such as £200 before pool money floating around, you cannot afford to approach a match in happy-go-lucky state of mind.

In this book I have tried to set down the specialist methods and techniques that are applied to match fishing. Some things are new, others are as old as fishing itself, but all are designed to do one thing—catch more fish. The approach of a matchman is so vastly different to that of the ordinary pleasure angler (not that match fishing is not very pleasurable) that it needs a book to explain it. In a match you have to win by any legitimate means you can. If you think you can win by catching tiny eels and rockling, then do so. It should be more pleasurable for you to weigh in 4 lb of dabs than a 3 lb 15 oz codling. If you can appreciate that, then you are well on the way to becoming a successful matchman.

Whether you are fishing in a small club match or the biggest open in the country, the idea is to win, and I hope to tell you how to do so.

In the book, I have taken it that the reader has a basic knowledge of casting and reeling in—this is not a book for beginners, but for the average angler who wants to develop his match fishing skills.

1

Fish and the Baits to Catch Them

Without any doubt, the right bait is one of the most important aspects of successful fishing. You can have the best rod and reel that money can buy, but with the wrong bait you might just as well be sitting in front of the fire as try to win a match.

There is more nonsense talked about fancy baits than about anything else these days, with anglers coming up with weirder and weirder combinations every week. The important thing to remember is that only a limited number of baits work successfully in any one place. The venues where fish will take anything offered to them are very few, and even in those places you will generally find that one bait will beat the rest. Because mussel is a good bait on the East coast of Yorkshire doesn't mean that the same bait would win a match (or even catch a fish) in Polperro. Too many anglers lay down the law about fishing baits saying this catches bass, that catches plaice, when, in truth, what is successful in one spot might be next to useless in another. If you can understand that what you use to catch fish on your own patch might not work somewhere fifty miles away then you are well on the road to becoming a successful match angler. Another important thing about baits is that just because a fish food is naturally plentiful on a beach does not mean it will make the best bait. It sounds nonsense, but I know several mussel beds where mussel is a poor bait and a river estuary that abounds with shrimp where no one would ever dream of using them for bait.

But there are exceptions to the rule. Ragworm usually fishes well over a ragworm bed and if you find a place where crabs abound and use it as bait you will score.

It is probably true to say that there are only a very limited number of baits that are any use to the match angler. Worms, crabs and fish are just about all you need to win any match, plus a little luck and experience.

I am deliberately not talking about each bait we know and what it *might* catch, but rather of each fish and what it usually takes. Far too often anglers talk about weird and wonderful selections of bait one of which will sometimes catch a fish. The matchman is concerned not with any fish but with the one that will win him the match by producing the heaviest weight of the day. The fact that some angler once caught a 10 lb skate on whelk, is not sufficient justification for recommending whelk as a good match bait.

The first great decision before any match is to decide what type of fish you want to catch and then try to fish exclusively for them. Figure out what fish are likely to be around and then pick the bait, for them. Never turn up with the bait just hoping it is the right one.

I will now list the main fish that the matchman is likely to meet and the baits that will *usually* take them. I stress the word *usually*, because there is nothing so unpredictable as fish and there are some venues where the fish feed on baits not generally associated with the specie. But, unless your experience tells you different, the following may be said to be true:

FLOUNDERS

Perhaps an odd fish to start off with you might think, but in many summer, autumn and winter matches it is the mainstay of the catches and produces the winning weight. The prime bait for flounders without any doubt is peeler crab and softback crab (henceforth I will refer to these two types of crab as simply 'crab' because there is little difference in the catching ability of each). I have caught flounder after flounder on crab, when worm anglers have been left fishless and probably plagued with crabs eating their bait the minute it touches the bottom. Crabs sometimes eat crab on the hook, but nowhere near as fast as they do worm. There are some places where crab does not fish well but these are usually well up-river where crab does not appear naturally, and at these places worm can fish well.

In these very brackish waters the fishing is exclusively, from the matchman's point of view, for flounders and eels. So if you are fishing a flounder spot that is well away from the sea, you would do well to have a few hours practice before the match, to see what bait catches fish there. It may well be lug or ragworm, or possibly even the very small 'creeper' rag.

If for some reason you cannot get crab, either because of bad weather or simply because it is winter then ragworm comes a good second for flounders. Unless I know a beach to be a real 'crab patch' then I always like to have some rag with me for flounders, if only for the odd flounder that takes a fancy to a change of diet. When there is crab in abundance, the flounders may well be so full up, that they go off crab slightly and may take worm just for the change. Lug is not really a flounder bait unless the match is being fished very high up river estuaries where sometimes it does win, but it is not the bait to win flounder matches with unless local knowledge tells you different.

Another word about those tiny harbour rag. These are the little worms that look like a baby rag and seldom exceed a couple of inches in length. They sometimes pay off for flounders in very cold weather when the shallow-water flounders are disinclined to feed on most other baits. I always reckon on March and April being the months for this flounder bait, when the fish have just returned from spawning and are in poor condition.

I have quite often used baited spoons and have a theory about them. Firstly, in a match where flounders are coming thick and fast they are of little use. The angler fishing three baited hooks will almost invariably take more fish than the chap with a single baited spoon. Secondly, I believe the spoon to be a method best used in clear water where the sunlight can catch the shiny surface and reflect it as it moves through the water. I know there is a school of thought which suggests that it is the vibration and not the flashing that attracts the flounder but I have yet to see it beat bait in muddy waters.

An odd bait that can catch flounders at times is shrimp. Either cooked or raw, pushed on the hook and gently cast (preferably off a pier where long casting is not needed), it can, at certain times of the year, take big bags of flounders. In one place I know shrimp is absolutely the only bait in Autumn for flounders and anglers have had winning match weights of 20 and even 30 pounds. But before any one tries shrimp in a match for flounders I would say test it in practice first. I do not like experimenting in a match.

EELS

Again a rather odd species to give prominence to, but in summer matches they can help in turning in a winning weight. Their advantage, like flounders, is that they are distributed practically all over the British Isles and especially where there are estuaries and harbours. I would also point out that the eel I am talking about here is the common eel that ascends the rivers to live in freshwater, not the conger eel.

Although many anglers curse the eel for the mess it can make of tackle, it is one of the hardest fish to catch. Anyone who thinks bass are hard to hook should try eel fishing when they are biting shy. It is the most frustrating thing there is when they just pull at the bait and never take it properly. Bootlace eels are even worse, the eel having a naturally small mouth. Before you scoff and ask who wants bootlace eels anyhow, remember that one eel could be the difference between first and second place. I have a very good friend and match angler, who lost an eel right at the edge of the water in a big Welsh beach open and was beaten into second place by a fraction of an ounce.

On eel baits I would say that eels are almost exclusively crab feeders. They do take worm, but only occasionally.

PLAICE

This fish is caught from early Spring right through to Autumn and can provide some useful backing weights for a catch of flounders and eels. It is rare to win a match exclusively with plaice, the only

The lazy, hazy fishing days of summer.

A bass comes to the gaff after being caught during a match on a spinner.

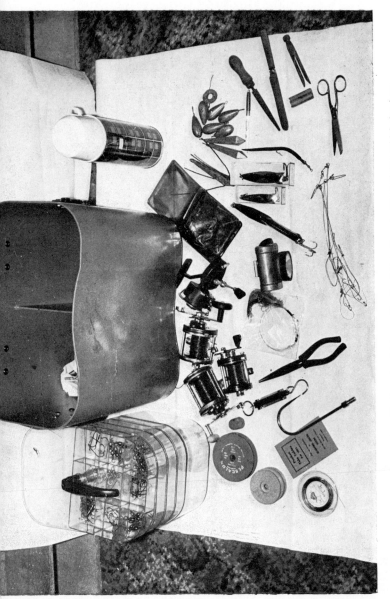

What every good tackle box should have. On the left is the plastic shelving which fits into one side of the box and the small compartments hold all the hooks and swivels you need. Other items (from left) are: steel trace wire, spool of 27lb line for tying hooks to, spool of 36lb for leaders, cork, tide table, gaff, spring balance, pliers, two big capacity reels and a narrow-spool reel, a spinning reel, mackerel feathers, bike lamp, stainless steel three-

exception being if you hit one big one of three or four pounds, and as they swim in the same waters as dabs, flounders and eels, they are a fish worth careful consideration by the sea matchman. The heaviest fish usually show at the beginning of the year and again at the back end.

Plaice feed naturally on small shellfish and tiny organisms in the sand for most of their life, which is why they are very often found on mussel beds and flat sandy beaches, although I have never found mussel to be a good bait for plaice. The plaice baits that consistently catch fish are lugworm and ragworm. Plaice are one of the few fish that do not take crab too well. Only fish upwards of $1\frac{1}{2}$ lb seem to take it, when they may do so in preference to worm baits, but as the match angler is usually concerned with quantity rather than quality then fish two worm-baited hooks and one crab-baited hook. In a match it is important to remember that usually a catch of small fish will beat the one big fish.

DABS

This is another of the mainstays of catches on sandy beaches and piers. They are also primarily worm feeders as opposed to fish baits or crab. Of the worms, lugworm caves high in the list and, if you can get it, the very big black worm known either as 'sewie' or 'Blackpool black' is excellent.

These big black worms are not the small ordinary lug that sometimes appear black but are about nine inches long which live in straight down burrows and need a special spade and technique to dig them.

I know of no place where any other bait will beat worm for dabs and unless you are fishing a match in a notoriously ragworm-only spot, I would put lug in front of rag for dabs.

Shellfish is a bait I have known take good match-winning bags of dabs but cockles and the like usually only fish well after a strong blow when plenty of shellfish have been washed up naturally and the fish have been feeding on them. Apart from instances such as this I would not recommend any shellfish as dab bait.

BASS

Certainly not a very predictable species at the best of times and definitely not the matchman's idea of an obliging fish. The trouble with bass is that there are so few of them ever caught in matches that the chance of cathing one through specialised fishing is very remote, hence it is never practical from a winning point of view to fish for bass in a match (unless it is a bass-only match). At the time of writing there is such a bass-only match held annually at Colwyn Bay in North Wales, where one bass netted a Southport angler £233.

These bass-only matches are invariably won with one large fish since the angler who can catch two bass in a match is either super-skilful or super-lucky, and probably the latter.

This is where the element of luck in sea matches shows itself most, because no matter how good an angler you are, if you are drawn in a spot that holds no bass you are out of luck—no other species will do.

However, should the match be bass-only then I recommend a two-hook trace (described in a later chapter) with crab on one hook and a local bait on the other. Crab is an almost universal bass-catching bait but use a local bait on the other hook for the odd bass that may fancy something different. I call local baits the one that is normally used to catch bass in that area—it may be ragworm, sprat or sandeel.

A bass match is one of the very few times when I would recommend using big hooks in a match. Depending on the size of the baits you are putting on I would be happy with anything up to 5/0 in fine wire hooks.

Spinning for bass in a match is a very sound approach for these fish and I once fished in a bass match over very rocky ground where my bottom-fished baits did nothing, while three anglers next to me with short spinning rods and Toby lures whipped out seven bass between four and seven pounds in a matter of an hour. This really opened my eyes to the potential of spinning for bass.

COD

In many areas this is the mainstay of catches all the year round, especially in the Northern waters from North East Yorkshire and the West of Scotland, the only difference in the fishing the whole year round being the size of the cod. It is generally true that summer fish are smaller than winter fish. It is probable that the summer fish live in the weed and rock edges all the year round and very often become a reddish colour as natural camouflage. They are then given localised names as rock cod, tangle cod and red cod. Codling are a good fish from the matchman's point of view because they are fairly plentiful and not too difficult to catch.

Baits for cod usually vary with the size of cod you are after. Never say in a blaze of pride 'I'm fishing for the double-figure fish' if it is unlikely there are any around. There are very few places indeed where you could make such a statement as that. The West of Scotland is one such place, but I honestly cannot bring to mind any other match venue where you can confidently expect to catch a double-figure cod from the beach. So fish for what you can honestly expect to catch and that means on average codling around the 2–4 lb range. We have all heard the weird and wonderful stories of things that have been found in the stomachs of cod from time to time, ranging from pebbles to plastic cups, but no one would dream of fishing with a plastic cup as bait! The match angler is only interested in the bait that will take the heaviest weight of cod and that narrows down the range tremendously.

I will divide cod baits up into two—Summer and Winter.

In Summer there is only one bait that has proved its consistency on every beach and that is crab. Other baits will catch fish but crab will catch the most, simply because of the terrific smell the bait has in the water. I defy anyone to show me a beach in summer where peeler crab will not catch cod and I know quite a few where crab is the only bait that *will* catch them. If I was due to fish a summer match where I knew codling would be the main quarry and I had no peeler crab, I would not go; it is as simple as that. All the other baits I list are second best baits—alternatives for a second or third hook when crab is on the first.

Optional Summer baits are: Lugworm, which I rate very poorly against crab. Ragworm, slightly better than lug on some beaches especially if it is found naturally there, but not as good as crab. Fish baits—in which I lump together things such as mackerel, herring, sprat, sandeel and pouting, worth putting on a third hook in case of a big lurker somewhere and useful in perhaps picking up a stray conger. Squid—again, sometimes a very useful second bait and one that has a strong smell to lure fish and is certainly an asset on most cod beaches. Trailing somewhat behind these in summer, there is mussel. I can hear the howls of disagreement now from the East where mussel is king but I fish the East Coast quite a lot in summer and although it will catch fish, it does not match up to crab.

The whole point of fishing in the sea is that you are not just catching enough fish for the tea table, you are out to beat a whole lot of other anglers who are just as keen as you to get in the prize list, so it is no good fishing with a second best bait and hoping to win. Granted you will take fish, but will you take enough? If mussel gives you confidence, then use it, but if you want to have a better chance of winning, have crab on as well and see which catches more fish.

For summer baits, therefore, crab is number one and the number two is rather up to you. It might be rag or lug or, perhaps, one of the fish baits.

These baits vary from place to place so just use your experience of venue to make a decision.

Turning to winter codling baits, the choice does get a bit more limited. If you live in the extreme South and West of England where it is possible to find at least a few crab right through winter, then lucky you! Crab is still number one. If like most of Britain your supply of crab peters out at the end of October when the cold and windy weather sets in, then you must turn elsewhere for your baits. With just the odd addition, the winter cod baits are the summer second choices. I cannot say which one is best, because what catches fish on one beach may not on another. What I can do, is to list again the baits you can choose from for cod in winter. The final choice must be left to your local knowledge.

They are: lugworm, ragworm, squid, fish and mussel. There are, I know many other baits that catch cod from time to time but I stress again the importance of fishing with the *best* bait, not just anything.

Winter is a time when I would try mussel as a bait. It is used almost exclusively on the East coast in winter for cod but it is worth a try in many other places. I have seen it catch cod on the fish-starved West coast of Lancashire when worm (the normal cod winter bait there) was drawing a blank, but I would not back it every time, even on the East coast. However, it is certainly worth putting on along with worm baits.

Shrimp is a very odd bait. I have spent hours and hours thinking about it as a bait and I must confess it still baffles me. Theoretically it should be the number one cod bait in winter in areas where shrimp abound, because on these shrimp beaches, every cod without exception is jam-packed full of them every time you catch them. It would seem, then, very logical to use shrimp as a successful hook bait. It is not quite so simple though—there are a few problems. Firstly, it is not an easy bait to hook on and keep on. It is fine if you are fishing on a pier where casting is not necessary, but on a beach it is usual to cast well out for day-time cod and the problem is in stopping the shrimps flying off in mid-air. It is frustrating to bait up several shrimps on a hook only to see them whistle off at the cast. But even if we overcome the problem of casting the bait, which would be possible with some thought (the new plastic that dissolves in water would be ideal for making bait bags) there is still another problem.

How do cod feed on shrimp naturally? I believe they find a dense shoal of shrimp, open their great mouths, and power their way through the shoal picking up every shrimp that is not fast enough to get out of the way. They probably never even deviate from a straight line—in a dense shoal of shrimp they do not need to—which is where the anglers' problem comes in. In all those millions of shrimps, what are the odds that a cod will pick up yours? Pretty slim, I think, and that is the great shrimp problem. But if you are experimentally-minded, then here is a great subject for research. I said earlier in this chapter that I have known shrimp to be a great bait for flounder and it could be the same for cod. Do not experiment in an actual match, however, but either before or after when you have the time.

WHITING

Whiting make a useful backing weight to a catch of winter dabs or codling, but the times when fishing for whiting is carried on to the exclusion of other fish is very rare so no specialised baits or techniques are really needed. The baits that take whiting are generally those that take cod, so even if whiting do make a show there is no need to change your bait.

DOGFISH

It is unfortunate that in many areas these fish tend to lie offshore and out of reach of the beach matchman, because if they shoaled regularly inshore it would be a wonderful opportunity for the matchman to use his speed—one of the best assets he has. If you are fishing a match where dogfish are a definite possibility, then do bait up one hook with fish bait in case one or two happen along—they make excellent weighing!

MACKEREL

Check up very carefully on match rules before fishing for mackerel. Many contests specifically bar them from being weighed in, which is rather a pity. Obviously, feathers are *the* lure for mackerel and I have no preference on colours—white or multi-coloured still catch mackerel. But if you do see a shoal of mackerel moving by make sure that in your haste to get the feathers out to them, you do not exceed the limit on the number of hooks allowed in the match. I must admit that I have only ever caught one mackerel in a beach match, and that, believe it or not, was caught on a bare hook about three feet from the edge!

SKATES AND RAYS

These, with the exception of thornback rays, tend to be very limited in distribution. Thornbacks are sometimes found on the beach but I cannot think of any occasion where I would try and fish exclusively for them from a beach; in fact, I do not think I would know how!

They tend to take fish baits usually, but the thornbacks I have caught from the beach have all been on crab while fishing for cod. They are certainly a match-winning fish if you can meet up with them. One thornback and you are in the prizes, two and the match is in the bag. So on baits for these fish, I would say if you are in an are a where they are likely, put fish or squid on one of the hooks, just in case.

CONGER

It takes a great deal of thought and plenty of local knowledge and luck to win a beach match with conger. I have seen beach matches won with a single conger in the Menai Straits in North Wales where the winner was shrewd enough to pick a known conger hideout and fish it exclusively all day with conger tackle. It was the real deep sea stuff—wire traces, 9/0 hooks and whole mackerel; it is a real do-or-die way of fishing a match. If you get a fish with this tackle you have won. But it is a gamble and you should be sure of your ground first. If you are drawn in a spot where conger are quite common then I say go ahead and fish for them exclusively. You just might crack it and it is certainly a good bet. Bait is obviously fresh mackerel, either a whole one or a good last.

POLLACK AND COALFISH

With these two fish, which have similar habits, a question of ethics arises. I am not myself such an ethical fellow (you have probably already grasped that), but in the lust for success it is prudent to pause when considering whether to go for pollack and coalfish. In many places these fish shoal densely around harbours and piers and have an average size of only a few inches. There are no statutory size limits for either of these fish and there are some contests—not many but some—that have no size limit at all on them. The result is that with the right light tackle you can take hundreds of these tiny fish in the course of a match and probably do very well in the prizes. But I think it is taking gamesmanship and professionalism too far. There is certainly some skill in taking a large quantity of these small fish, but is it really ethical?

Even from the conservation point of view it is not really giving these small fellows much of a look at life in the sea. If you *want* to fish for these tiny pollack and coalfish and the contest rules allow it, then go ahead, and the best of luck to you.

However, bigger pollack and coalfish are a more interesting proposition. Above ten inches (the generally accepted minimum size for these fish in most matches) they can be a good source of weight and knowing a bit about them is an advantage in a match. They feed on almost anything—see the section on cod baits with a little less emphasis on the fish baits. In summer, pollack and coalfish very often shoal near the surface quite close in and if you are ever fishing a match and this happens, you could think about spinning with a toby lure, or something similar. When they do come to the surface on the West coast of Scotland it is almost like the evening rise on a trout lake. They flip and roll making rings on the surface, just like a trout taking flies and if you do get the chance to spin for them then go ahead, providing there is nothing in the match rules of the day which prohibits spinning. The lures are many and varied, but you will not go far wrong if you stick to the toby and krill lures.

HADDOCK

The only place you can hope to catch these from the shore is in the West of Scotland and they are not worth fishing for exclusively even there. If you must, they take all the standard cod baits.

WRASSE

The matches where you could seriously fish for wrasse are very few and far between and probably the majority of anglers have never even caught one, but these little fellows are quite common around rocky shores. If the place you are in is noted for producing wrasse of any kind, then you could pull off a surprise victory by forgetting the other fish around and fishing for them exclusively. I know it seems an odd thing to do, but it is these little tricks that make successful matchmen. Baits for wrasse are shellfish, crabs and worms. Try a bit of each till you hit them.

TOPE

A fish not very commonly fished for from the beach and hence not very often caught, but there are places where match fishing for tope is promising. In North Wales the art of tope fishing has been explored to some extent by Bruce McMillen who has made some remarkable catches of these fish from the beach using big fish baits but the kind of tope fishing from the beach that interests me is of a different kind. The smaller tope—those up to a couple of pounds—very often swim close in after a calm spell in summer and early autumn and catching them is definitely worth while. I am, at the time of writing plotting such a course of action in several big opens in the near future because you only need a couple of these small tope and you can smile all the way to the prize table. Although in the summer months they will take crab, my plan is to fish for them with smallish lasts of fresh mackerel on a trace that has crab on for all the ordinary summer species.

CONCLUSION

Any fish I have not yet mentioned is really a match oddity or rarity. Fish such as gurnards, rockling, sea scorpions, soles and mullet are caught from time to time, but they are never worth fishing for seriously. Either you have not the time, as with mullet; or there are not enough of them, such as scorpions. In any case, many of these smaller species are specifically not allowed in some contests, so before you try and weigh one in, you had better check that doing so will not get you barred.

2

The Collecting and Presentation of Baits

Presentation is definitely one of the secrets of success in all aspects of fishing, and nowhere more so than in competitive fishing. It might be easy to catch a couple of fish using haphazard methods and presentation, but you will not catch a lot, consistently, with shoddy baits.

The golden rule of bait presentation is that it should not only look right, it should *smell* right too. One of those bones of angling contention is whether fish hunt by sight or smell. I believe that different species act differently towards sight and smell but the important thing is that *all* fish hunt by smell to some degree, so smell is important. A fish can live if it is blind, but it has no chance if it cannot smell!

So, rule number one—put fresh bait on at every cast if possible. The usual reason for it being impossible is if, through bad management and planning, you have not brought enough. The advantages of such a smart move as this, hardly need explaining, but it is surprising the number of good anglers who do not do it. The only reason for not making a change at every cast is laziness; laziness in not getting the bait or making the effort of taking off the old and putting on the new. This kind of match angler never makes the top—in fact never quite makes anything. I will next list all the baits mentioned in the previous chapter and how to obtain and present them. I will start off with the one factor to which I attribute whatever success I have had in the past and whatever successes I might have in the future. In a word, CRAB.

CRAB

Whether it is peeler or softback, it is deadly in England, Ireland, Scotland and Wales and no trophies are safe when there are anglers using this bait correctly. However, for some reason there seem to be very few (if any) angling writers who seem to have a proper understanding of the bait. I am forced to smile when I read of people tying on crab with cotton and elastic thread; and there are even some weird contraptions called crab hooks—rather like double hooks with safety pins attached—that are sold as the answer to keeping this soft bait on the hook while casting.

I must confess here and now that I do not know how to tie crab onto a hook or use one of these safety pin gadgets (not that I would ever want to) because I have learnt a little of the art of crab fishing of which first lesson is putting it on the hook. It is possible to put either peeler or softback crab on the hook without tying with cottons and rubber bands. I want to see the mystique surrounding peeler crab exploded once and for all. There is nothing secret or difficult about crab fishing once you know the basic rules of it given in the following pages.

For the technically minded, shore crabs can be divided up into many different types with scientific names but, simply, there are the ordinary crabs which so love to eat baits in summer and are what we might call the standard type crab, coming in different colours, ranging from bright green to bright red; the edible crabs—those which adorn shellfish shop windows; and the rarer spider, velvet and porcelain crabs.

I know there are a few more different types swimming around, but these are the most common types and of these, two only are really of interest to the angler. These two are the hermit crab and the common crab. I know there are some anglers who will disagree, but I do not like either spiders or porcelain crabs for bait. I have used porcelain crabs in the past and found them a poor substitute for the common variety. I have never found a peeler or softback spider crab and, for that matter, I do not want to.

Recognising the different types of crabs is not very difficult: there is the ordinary shore crab which comes in quite a few colours, ranging from red to whitey grey; the porcelain crab I know better as the swimmer crab. We call it a swimmer because of the little paddles on its back legs which it uses for fast swimming. These crabs look almost as though they are made out of porcelain and are a pure white underneath and a sandy brown on the back. They are the only crab I have come across which is downright vicious, sometimes hanging on with their nippers to your thumb till they draw blood. They are more often found at the edge of the water, rather than in pools and under seaweed where normal crabbing is carried on. The edible crabs are oval in shape, rather lethargic and purplish in colour, with short fat hairy legs. Spider crabs look as they sound—like a spider with long hairy legs and a little head.

Coming back to the crab the angler is mainly concerned with— the shore crab—there are two names for the two stages of its life that interest anglers—peeler and softback. As a crab grows its shell does not so every now and then it grows a new shell. It does this by forming the new shell underneath while the old one is still on top, and when the time to get rid of the old one comes, the crab takes in water, swelling itself bursting the old shell and exposing the new. The new shell when it first emerges is soft and requires time to harden up and it is while it is in this soft stage that the crab is most vulnerable and so hides away before it sheds (or peels) its old shell.

When the crab is about to shed the old shell with the new soft one underneath it reaches the stage we call peeling and so a peeler crab is one that is about to shed its old shell. A softback crab is one that already has shed the old shell and whose new shell has not yet hardened up. There is a further stage when the soft shell has begun to harden up and we call this a crackly, crispie or crinkly (sounds like a breakfast cereal) crab, because the shell feels slightly crisp. Beyond this stage the crab is of no use to the angler.

While it is easy to recognise a softie, peelers can be a bit more difficult but with practice becomes child's play. The first problem in crabbing is to know where to find them. Remember that they are going to be very easy prey for fish when they have peeled, so they will be hidden away somewhere underneath old pipes, rocks, seaweed and round pier piles.

You will never get a peeler crab being caught on rod and line so do not investigate every crab you pull up from the pier. They are not interested in eating while they are in the peeling stage. Every beach has different crab hiding places but if you have any of the following features on your local beach, then look there for your crabs:

Walls that have a seaweed skirt on them: These are usually harbour walls where the seaweed runs along the base of the wall and provides first class cover for the crabs. A tip for finding crabs in these conditions is not just to lift the seaweed and look, but to scrape along the sand under the weed with your fingers and feel for them, as very often the crabs will not just hide behind the weed, but actually bury themselves in the sand as well. To save you wasting time looking in places where crab are very unlikely to be found remember the golden rule of crabbing—there must be plenty of moisture in the sand where you are looking. Crabs need water so they will always hide in a place that has a ready supply such as a rock pool or somewhere very wet or muddy.

Harbours are very good for a supply of crabs and there are plenty of places within a harbour worth rooting round. Look for old drums, sheets of corrugated iron, old fish boxes, in fact anything that might possibly hide a crab, turn them over and scratch through the sand.

Breakwaters are another very productive source of crabs. It rather depends on their construction but many are so built that wind and tide have formed crevices underneath the breakwater where crabs lie in droves. If there is water surrounding the end of a breakwater, then it is certainly worth rooting about, but try to feel right under the breakwater where the best crabs will be hiding. Breakwater crabs are sometimes a bit cunning and will do their utmost to fool you into thinking there are only hardbacks under that breakwater.

They do this in a very cunning way by pushing all the softback and peeler crabs to the back while the hardback crabs stand at the front trying to fight you off. So the first thing that happens is that you keep pulling hardback after hardback out when the peeler crabs hope you will go away in despair. The shrewd crabber keeps on pulling out these hardbacks from under the breakwater until at last, you begin to pull out prime peelers. Once you have cleared out all the hardbacks from under a breakwater (and they might be upwards of sixty guarding their brothers) you very often find that you cannot get anything else but peelers and from one breakwater you can get as many as you need. It is unwise to go quickly from breakwater to breakwater pulling out just a few crabs at a time. You get one or two peelers this way but by far the majority are missed.

A sewer-pipe is another good crab-producing place. I know many anglers turn up their noses at putting their hands around these evil-smelling places but they are often goldmines of peelers. To crab a sewer pipe look for one with some water around it and, where the water meets the pipe, begin digging your hands in the sand and running your fingers quickly over the sides of the pipe under water. I emphasise speed because as soon as the crab feels your hand moving through the water he shoots off. Other good places around sewer pipes are underneath, where the pipe meets the sand. Scratch about in the sand here and you will find quite a few crabs.

Piers and iron jetties are an excellent source of crabs and, again, the rule is look for water and cover. Where the sand is very wet and sloppy around the piles, you can dig in the sand around the piles, going round the post till it is done. Where the piles lie in a pool, as is often the case towards the end, a different technique is needed. The procedure is to run both hands quickly down the side of the post feeling for crabs on the way. If nothing is felt, then run your hands all around the post and, if still nothing, go to the bottom of the post and run your hands around the bottom to see if any are trying to bury themselves in the sand. If there are still no crabs then it is fair to say there are none around that post. Crabbing in this manner I have had as many as three hundred and fifty in a matter of hours.

Rocks and pools are equally as good as piers and the manner of crabbing them is by brute strength. Look for a rock (usually a biggish one) that looks as though it could hide a crab under it, lift it and look. If the sand is very sloppy under the rock, then give it a quick scrape with your fingers to check that there are none hiding under the sand. It is hard to describe the kind of rocks that crabs like, but after a while, you begin to know the right kind. Just remember the rule of cover and moisture.

There are, of course, other places that produce crabs such as wrecks and slipways, but most beaches should have one of the things I have listed for crabbing. If you find other places to crab then jolly good luck to you.

There are many anglers who have a great fear of the unknown in putting their hands in dark murky pools where they cannot see the bottom, worried that something might grab hold of their hand while it is under the water. There is not much you can do if you are such an angler except to crab places where you do not have to put your hand in pools of water, or to wear rubber gloves. I have known people who were shy of putting their bare hands in a pool become quite good crabbers by wearing rubber gloves and, if nothing else, they may protect you from cuts on pieces of rusty metal or broken glass. But one habit I never like to see is the use of garden rakes and shrimp nets. Not only do you miss most of the crabs but you could stab otherwise healthy crabs, reducing the stocks.

Crabbing is best carried out on your own. There is a fresh influx of peelers at every tide but if someone has been down before you you will have a hard time of it. The first angler crabbing always takes the easy crabs and leaves a few of the more inaccessible ones. So obviously, the first one gets the pick and the most, which gives us another golden rule of crabbing—get there first as soon as the tide ebbs at your crabbing spot.

As to recognising peelers and softbacks when you find them, I do not think anyone should have any trouble in telling a softback crab when he finds it for the simple reason that it is soft! With peeleers, it is important to realise that they go through several stages before actually peeling and it is the stage just before the final shedding of the shell that the crab is at its best for fishing. This is when the old shell is very fragile and easy for the angler to take off when fishing. To test a crab to see if it is a peeler take hold of one of the legs and gently twist and pull at the very end joint. If this pulls off clean, leaving nothing underneath but a piece of white gristle, then it is not a peeler. Put it back to grow another leg. If the end of the leg shell comes off revealing a firm, soft leg underneath of a brownish-yellow colour (or even black) then this is a peeler. Put him in the bucket.

It is not easy to describe on paper the difference between the legs of hardback crabs and peelers, but once you have had a couple of hours crabbing and seen the two, it becomes simple. I emphasise the importance of twisting and pulling gently, or you will pull off the whole leg every time, whether the crab is a peeler or not. If you think you may have done this then try again with another leg, but have a little pity for the crab and do not pull every leg off. Alternatively, you can test one of the nippers. Take a firm hold of the top half of the crab nipper that moves up and down and gently break it off. If it, too, shows a firm dark piece of flesh underneath then that is a peeler. If it comes off with a flaky white piece of tissue then it is a hardback.

If you examine all the peelers you find you will see that some are actually in the process of losing their old shell and you should see a big split between the back and the belly—this is how the crab sheds its shell. It takes in water, swelling out till it literally bursts its sides. From the moment the crab actually starts to swell to having lost the old shell is quite fast and does not take more than five or ten minutes. I have watched crabs peeling on many occasions and it is a fascinating process. They slowly and painstakingly pull themselves out of the shell and lie quite exhausted beside it. It is when

they have just peeled that the crabs are at their weakest and they can
hardly move for a day or two till the new shell begins to harden
and they get back some strength. When you find a crab that has
just peeled—we call them jelly softies—you must treat it like a baby
if you want to keep it; if you just throw it in with the rest of the
crabs it will get crushed underfoot.

Another way you can sometimes tell peelers is by watching out
for carriers. These are two crabs that are mounted with each other,
usually a big crab holding a smaller one underneath him with his
claws. The one underneath is usually either a softback or a peeler
and the one above a hardback.

A few words now about crabbing and temperature. Crabs are
very susceptible to weather changes and it is a sure sign of stormy
weather ahead when the crabs suddenly disappear. They are
also reluctant to peel when there is a wind blowing because, I
suppose, they are afraid of being washed out of their holes with no
protection. During a prolonged spell of windy weather it can be a
nightmare trying to get enough crab to fish a big match and many
times I have spent three days crabbing for one three-hour match.
They are also affected by temperature changes and when it begins
to cool down they hibernate, or at least disappear from the rocks
and piers.

In the North where I crab and fish mostly, the crab season starts
with the onset of the warmer weather usually about the first week
in May and continues until the first frosts or stormy weather in
either early or late October.

I know that some lucky anglers can get crab all the year round in
the South and West of England, but for most of the country the
times when you can get crab are those I have described. There
are also certain times of the year when you can get a glut of crab.
We call these the 'first big peel' and the 'last big peel'. The first
big peel usually occurs in mid-June and it is possible to get hundreds
of crab in this balmy month. Then the crabbing becomes a little
harder until autumn when there is the last big peel as the crabs shed
their shells for the last time before winter. If you crab regularly and

The author's method of fingering for bites.

Fishing at the Seaham, Co. Durham, Open – the first in Britain to top the 2,000 entry mark.

The last stage of peeling a crab and taking off the back shell.

After peeling, cut the crab in half.

can recognise this last big peel when it comes, it is a sure sign that the crabs are going to get very scarce very soon and it is wise to build up a big stock when this happens.

Now for keeping crabs: there are two schools of thought on this and both work well. First there is the wet method which involves the use of fresh seaweed. Use a large box with a firm lid, line well with wet fresh seaweed and keep in a cool place. A refinement on this is to put the crabs in a seaweed box and put the box in the fridge to keep very cool.

Temperature is very important in keeping crabs; the best way I know of killing crabs is to let them get too warm. The ideal figure for keeping crabs is between 40°F and 45°F. This is not so cold that they freeze nor so warm as to kill them. Ideally get your own fridge solely for storing bait, not only for keeping crab in summer but for keeping winter baits such as fish and worms as well.

Perhaps you have an understanding wife or mother who does not mind you using the household fridge for storing crabs, but such women are rare. The secret of keeping crabs alive using the wet method is to keep changing the seaweed and not to let it go off. I would not recommend keeping seaweed for longer than three days—if it goes off, it will kill the crabs quicker than anything.

Incidentally, I read in an angling journal recently that it was inadvisable to keep peelers and softbacks in the same box as the former will kill the latter. What bunkum! I have been keeping crabs for many years now and I have yet to see two crabs fight. In fact—quite the opposite—crabs *protect* each other.

The second method of keeping crabs is the dry method. One factor that it has in common with the wet method is that temperature plays an important part. To keep crabs using the dry method you also need a box with a lid but you put the crabs in dry and keep them at a temperature not below 40°F. If the temperature drops much below this the crabs will freeze to death. It is a strange sight to see a crab that has frozen to death; its legs are stretched out almost straight and it looks as though it has really shivered.

Just to confuse the issue, there is a third way of keeping crabs that combines both methods. Keep the crabs in a dry box but lay a piece of wet sacking on them. Wet, I hasten to add, with seawater *not* freshwater. If you use damp sacking re-wet the sack every three days or the water will go sour and possibly kill some of the crabs.

I have mentioned all methods of keeping crabs because the place you live obviously affects the method. If you live twenty miles. inland you can hardly go to the coast three times a week just to wet a sack, so you would use the dry method. But if you live on the coast you would probably use the wet method.

One important thing with all methods is to check all the crab stock at least every day to sort out the dead ones. Do not get too despondent if you always seem to lose your biggest and best peelers while the crackly ones and peelers that are a long way off being ready live for ever. The reason for this is that crabs will not peel unless they think they are safe from predators and bad conditions— and that includes being stuffed in dark boxes. The crab, when it peels, takes in a large volume of water which expands the body under the shell and causes the old shell to burst open and allow the soft crab to crawl out, so quite obviously if there is no water and no security the crab will not peel and so dies.

The latest advances in crab fishing have involved the deep freezing of peelers in summer when they are plentiful and saving them for winter when they are scarce or non-existent. I cannot give any definite ruling on this yet as it is still at the trial stage, but there is obviously a tremendous advantage in having such superb bait when no one else has. The snag is whether fish will take it readily in winter? I say this because it is hardly a natural bait in winter when most of the crab population is hibernating and what few are pottering about are feeding so slowly as not to need to peel. But, nevertheless, I feel that deep-frozen crab used in winter will catch cod and if you are one of the growing number of households who have a deep freeze then wrap the crabs individually in polythene, whole and with all the legs and nippers intact, and store them away until winter.

Keeping crab on the beach is a bigger problem than you might think. The tendency is to stuff about fifty or so in a bag and leave them at the bottom of the basket until the day is over. The snag with this is that if the hot sun shines on the bag, those crabs will bake alive and will all be dead before the match is half over. Apart from wanting them to last the match alive you naturally would like to save what is left for the next match.

The method I have adopted now and which is working admirably is to use a box with a polystyrene lining which keeps the crabs cool even in the hottest sun. The principle of polystyrene is that it reflects the sunlight shining on it and when the coolness of the crabs inside the box reflects onto the polystyrene that too bounces back, keeping the hot out and the cold in. An added coolant is to have a piece of wet sacking on top of the crabs in the box with the lid firmly closed. If you are practically inclined you might also line your crab box at home with polystyrene.

Moving on from keeping crab to actually using it, the two essentials (apart from a bagful of crab) are a flat board about a foot square, henceforth referred to as the crab board, and a very sharp knife.

You will notice as you become familiar with crab fishing that there are some crabs which seem easier to peel than others and the reason for this is that prior to peeling the shell becomes brittle and loose and will literally fall off. I said earlier that crabs take in water just before they peel. Because the crab flesh is so fluid when put on the hook this type of peeler is packed with fish-attracting juice and will fish better than crabs that are not quite ready, and they are easier to peel in this state. To find out if a crab will peel easily, pick it up and look at the shell between the belly and the back shell underneath the nippers. This is the first part of the shell to split naturally and if you can see a hairline crack or a gaping hole here then that is a prime crab.

Crabs that crack when you lightly press on that area are just as good. The shell on all true peelers will come off but finding the ones just about to peel makes the job so much easier.

Having selected the best crab to use strip off all the shell on the crab and begin pulling off all the legs and nippers. Put them on a corner of the crab board for use later. Begin by prising off with your fingernail the triangular piece of shell that covers the crab's bottom. Then take off that shell on the belly and the side flaps and lastly prise off the shell back, but gently so as not to break up the crab. Place it on the crab board and cut it in half from front to back and you will see the yellowy juices that are so attractive to fish. Peel the legs by taking them between forefinger and thumb and gently twisting and pulling on one segment at a time. The order you take the shell from the leg does not matter just so long as you do it gently. You can peel nippers in much the same way.

To hook the crab start by pushing the hook point through the front part of the crab from top to bottom, a little way from the front of the crab, and bring it through the other side. Then push the hook through the crab again till the hook again comes through the other side. If the size of the crab warrants it, push it through again till the crab has been threaded up the hook and the hook point is at the bottom end of the crab.

It certainly does not look like a crab now but, by golly, it smells like one. Most fish hunt primarily by smell rather than sight, so it is more important for a bait to smell right rather than to look right. Next take a couple of peeled crab legs and push them onto the hook point. This will help keep the piece of crab well up the hook and will not mask the point when you strike.

The same procedure applies to using softback crabs (remember to take all the legs off) and keep it on by using peeler legs instead of softback crab legs. Although this method will keep softies on quite well obviously you cannot expect to punch the weight out great distances, but you do not need to in many cases, as I shall be explaining later.

In a match it is good practice and time-saving to have always three or four pieces of crab always peeled and cut up at any one time and a plentiful supply of peeled legs.

RAGWORM

Over the year I would be tempted to rate this as the number two bait for the match angler. There are not many fish that will not readily take it, and, what is more important, a lot of fish prefer it to other worm baits. Using it is nowhere near as complicated as crab, but, nevertheless, there are certain rules you have to follow to succeed with it.

Digging ragworm is more back breaking than difficult because the type of ground that ragworm love is usually pebbly, rocky or, at the best, tightly packed mussel. The type of fork to use for ragworm should ideally be as long as possible in the tines (that is the technical word for prongs). My local ironmonger calls the type I buy, potato forks, but go into any good garden shop and you should easily spot the bigger ones. Avoid at all cost those little forks that are meant for pottering in the potting shed—they cost too much time in lost worms.

The kind of ground to look for when rag digging, is either mussels, pebbles and sand inter-mixed, or tightly packed clay. But reputation is a better guide really. Just about every decent rag bed in the British Isles is known so if you want to dig your own rag, ask around.

If the rag bed is a very good one and the worms are thick you can begin digging where you fancy (near a pool of water is a good place) and trench along till you hit them. Trenching is a regulated way of digging. If you are on your own you dig three or four forkfuls out in a line in front of you and then work progressively backwards keeping the trench about four forkfuls wide.

If the ground is very wet and your trench keeps flooding, then narrow it to a couple of forkfuls wide.

If you are on a bed that has been well hammered and the worms are there but far from plenty, you will save a lot of time and work by 'treading' for individual worms. You do this by looking for a little of jet water about an eighth of an inch wide spurting out of the ground when you tread near it. This spurt is coming from the ragworm who lies in a long burrow. The tread is more of a shuffle, really. You stamp and shuffle along, your eyes looking at the ground immediately in front of you. Do not be fooled by very tiny jets of water that shoot up by the hundred. That is not a fantastic rag bed you have discovered but a mass of tiny rag that is no good to anyone. Look for the big jets of water; once you have seen one you will easily recognise it again. As you dig probably the first sign of a worm you will see is either a big hole going through the ground or a fast-disappearing tail. The course of action in both cases is the same: dig furiously in the direction of the hole or where the worm is travelling. Under no circumstances grab hold of the tail and try and pull out the worm. The only result will be that at the end of the day you will have a bucket full of rag tails. The worm will break if you pull with any pressure at all. It is far better to try and dig the worm out or at least expose the best part of it. The amount of rag you will need for a match depends on what fish you are after, how many you expect to catch, and how many other baits you have as well, but as a general guide if the worms are about eight or nine inches long (which is about average) for a four hour match where it was intended to be the main bait for codling, I would not feel happy with less than two dozen. If the rag is supplementing a bag of crab then a dozen is sufficient. Do not get into the habit of digging up a hundred or so for a three hour club match. It is exactly this practice that has put paid to one of the best rag beds I know around my area. Storing ragworm is not difficult provided you keep it cool and dry. The best way is to wrap the worms up individually in clean newspaper and then either put them at the bottom of the fridge or in some cool place. Check the paper every day to see that it has not got damp. Damp paper is about the best way of killing ragworm.

I cannot recommend buying ragworm from a tackle shop. The number of shops that sell locally-dug ragworm seem to be on the decrease and more and more ragworm are being shipped across the Irish Sea these days. It is not the diggers' of the dealers' fault but by the time the angler actually gets to put these shop-bought worms on the hook they may be anything up to a week old and they look limp, lifeless, tasteless and travel-sick. If at all possible, dig your own.

Freshness is important with all baits but none more so than rag. Apart from anything else, the shop-bought packets usually contain only a couple of good worms, the rest being small worms—hardly value for money.

There is only one successful way of hooking on ragworm and that is right down the middle. Break off a piece that will cover the hook shank with about 2 inches pushed up the line for flatfish and about four inches for small codling, whiting, etc. If you have plenty of rag and are going after codling over the 3 lb mark then push on a full rag. But do not be misled into thinking that you will stand a better chance of more flatties with a wacking great piece of worm on the hook. You will probably get plenty of bites as the fish suck at the bait with their tiny mouths but you will miss a lot. Only with fish such as codling, which seem to have a gulp-now, think-later reasoning, can you do that and score.

A bad method of hooking rag is passing it in and out of the worm at three points so that, in theory, the worm waves about in a natural wriggle. In practice, the worms slide down to form a big lump on the hook—most unnatural. Another bad match practice is to use a tiny hook, say a freshwater size 14, above the hook to hold the rag up the line and to prevent it from slipping down the line. It may well succeed in holding up the rag, but remember that most contests allow only three hooks and so a two-hook trace, which with this tandem method would actually have four hooks in the water, you would be risking disqualification. If you find the worm is slipping down the hook and forming a blob it is better to use the worm stop knot on the line—something I shall be talking about in a later chapter.

LUGWORM

There are two kinds of lugworm used by sea anglers. The most common one is the small brownish one that you can dig up with a garden fork and whose casts sometimes cover whole stretches of beach. The other one is what I call black; it looks structurally the same as a lug but is much bigger, growing sometimes to nine inches, and is a lot fatter. Usually it is jet black, but sometimes a brownish-red colour and as short as five inches. The most obvious way to tell the two types apart, however, is that you buy lug alive and you buy black dead. Blackworms are called 'sewie' and 'gully' worms in different parts of the country but, because they are not as widely distributed as the orindary small lug on the beaches, you may not have come across them before.

The reason that the black are dead when you use them is quite simple. If you did not kill them when you dug them, the worms would kill themselves. The worm when dug out and laid on the beach or in a bucket would simply force all the fluid in its body up to the head and burst open. So, as a matter of ease of handling, as soon as black are dug out they are 'knocked' on the spade handle.

If you are buying worms from a shop then a very simple guide as to which are ordinary lug and which are black is the price. Lug are usually about 15p a dozen whereas black will be at least 45p a dozen.

To dig ordinary lug you need a fork, a bucket and a broad back. For anyone who does not know what a lug cast looks like, it is that curly wisp of sand that lies on the beach. Find a stretch of beach where the lug casts are quite thick and commence to dig. The method to use is trenching, which is a methodical and systematicaly uplifting of the sand designed to take the maximum of worms with the minimum of effort. If you are on your own you can dig in much the same way and style as I described earlier for ragworm and again, if at four forkfuls wide your trench is continually flooded, block off the sides where the water is coming in and drop down to three forkfuls wide.

The big secret in lug digging is to stick at one trench and not to keep moving after half a dozen digs. If you have stopped getting worms after a while then by all means move, but give each trench a fair try.

To keep lug you need somewhere cool and lots of dry newspapers. Spread out a sheet of newspaper and lay out the lug on it so that they are not touching each other and have a bit of elbow room.

Then lay on top of that a couple of thicknesses of paper and start again, building up the layers until all the worms are covered. I use an old tomato box for keeping mine in for ease of carrying but, as long as they cannot get out, anything will do. Check the paper each day to see if any of the worms have blown. You will know exactly what I mean by blown the first time you see one. The lug head goes to jelly and is quite dead. If you do not throw it out it will smell, too. It is a good idea to change the paper every day or more often if it gets damp. Damp paper kills lug quickly. To store them for a few days either put them in the fridge or keep them somewhere cool. In winter they should keep fairly well for four or five days, but it is much harder in summer when they can go off in a day.

As for hooking lugworm, it all depends on the size of the worms you are using. If the worms you are getting are about five inches long from head to tail these make a nice hookbait for flatfish. I know you cannot predict the size of lug you are going to dig but it is fairly common to find that in a bed all the worms are about the same size, so if you are getting those tiny lug, only about two or three inches long, find somewhere else to dig. If you cannot get anything but small lug then put two on a hook.

I hook lug not in the conventional manner of pushing the hook through the head, threading it down the line and pushing the hook through the tail, but by starting the other way round and baiting the lug beginning at the tail. Still thread it along the line but as the point comes out at the head instead of the tail you get less loss of juices by breaking the worm. You will notice if you thread a lug starting at the head that the eye of the hook as it is forced through the flesh has a tendency to split open the worm and the guts, which by their smell help to attract the fish, drip out before the worm is in the water. By hooking the worm from the back only, the hook point is pushed through the head and, therefore, you get less spillage. If you are using two lug to a hook then obviously you just push one right the way up the hook and thread the second one underneath it.

For flatfish and small roundfish one good lug makes a perfect bait, but if you are going after cod, two or even three big worms is the style. As I have said, cod are like marine vacuum cleaners and the more bait they see the greedier they get.

One important point with lug is to change the worm at every cast. You will get through an awful lot of worms this way I know, but if you want to win you must have the maximum chance of catching fish. You want a bait that has as much smell as possible.

Now the big black lug. Digging these fellows is a fine art and unless you know what you are doing you will find it heartbreaking. To start with you can forget digging with a fork. You need a very thin bladed spade that can dig sand out fast to catch the swift-moving worm.

The black stretches out to a great length as it lies in its U-shaped burrow and, as soon as it feels disturbance overhead, it begins to contract which gives it the appearance of burrowing very fast. The worm can burrow in sloppy sand quite quickly but not fast enough to beat a flashing blade. To recognise the black cast as distinct from the lug cast is not easy at first. The black cast is a shorter thicker coil of sand, anything up to one eighth of an inch thick. The best thing to do is to find out where these big worms can be dug (there are not that many places), go down on a big ebb and watch some diggers at work. You will soon see the kind of cast they are picking out as black, but I think you might find some sour comments if you try to pick these diggers' brains. There is a lot of money to be earned at this game and those who are in it are naturally reluctant to encourage anyone else to dig them.

But I will presume that you have got a good idea of what a black cast looks like and where you can dig them. To commence digging, position yourself about a couple of feet behind the cast and start to dig a narrow trench about two thin spades wide about six inches in front of the cast. Angle your digs at about 45° and dig quickly and cleanly, leaving as little sand in the hole as possible. Work towards the cast still keeping at the 45° angle. By this time you should have sighted the large burrow hole, and as soon as you do see it dig quickly, straight down after the worm and expose part of it. As soon as you have seen the worm and know exactly where it is, dive down the hole with your hand and feel in the sand for the worm. If you cannot feel the worm straight away feel around for the burrow hole and work your hand through it and further down it until you can get a firm grip with your fingers on part of it. Do not under any circumstances try to pull the worm out quickly or you will snap it and lose all but the tail. Gently ease the worm out, pulling until you feel it come free. After a while you should be able to judge just exactly how much pressure you can put on the worm and should break very few. As soon as you have pulled the worm out, take it between the finger and thumb at about the middle of the worm and give the head of the worm some violent knocks on the spade handle to burst the guts out.

Although it sounds quite easy, blackworm digging is a fine art and it takes a long while to get used to the method. Apart from that, as I said earlier, they are only found in certain parts of the country.

To keep black fresh wrap them up in dry newspaper separately and keep them cool. You can tell when they are going off by the smell!

They fish well for dabs and sometimes whiting and codling and for dabs you only need a piece about two inches long threaded on the hook. For codling, you can push a whole worm on the hook with a worm stop knot to hold it up the hook.

FISHSTRIP

This is not a bait that comes very high on my list of top baits, but for certain species it is deadly. As the fish you are usually aiming for with fishstrip are big fish—conger, skate, etc., you naturally have larger hooks on which helps tremendously in keeping this bait on.

I honestly do not think there is much difference between herring and mackerel as long as both are fresh. Shop-bought fish would be a last resort for me—mackerel caught the same or previous day are much more appetising to the fish. To prepare a strip of mackerel get a sharp knife and run it along the flank of the fish and there you have the strip or 'last' of fish as it is sometimes called.

Because of the bait's softness it does not cast very well, so exercise care with it. One idea I have been trying out lately with fish strip, is using a tandem of two hooks, one tied on the line just above the other. By having the mackerel hooked on in two places there is a better chance of it staying on and it possibly increases your hooking chances too.

One important thing to remember with strip is to make sure that the hook point is showing, so that when you strike the pull is not cushioned by the flesh of the bait. But, I repeat, the main concern with fishstrip is that it be as fresh as possible.

SQUID

Squid is fast becoming an 'in bait' and at the time of writing I am experimenting with it. Up until recently, the use of squid as a bait seems to have been reserved for the South coast but as other baits get scarcer squid has been creeping up North.

The first time I saw a match won with it was on The Gareloch, which runs into the Clyde, and how it came to win the match was a pure fluke. The day before the match I had been wandering round the nearby town of Helensburgh looking for a newsagent when I came across a wet fish shop that had a whole squid lying in the window. More out of curiosity than experience I went in and bought it and took it along to the match the next day. A couple of chums who were with me reluctantly baited up with this squid, along with a couple of hooks with peeler crab on, and we cast out. Within minutes—bang! One of the lads was into a 6¼ lb thornback —needless to say caught on squid.

Five minutes later the other was into a 8¼ lb conger—on squid. These were the only two fish caught on the bait—the rest of the time we caught small codling on crab—but these two fish gave first and second place to their captors.

Using this bait is simple. Gauge the amount of bait in proportion to the mouth of the fish you are after. With flatfish cut long thin strips and for bigger species, such as cod and doggies, chunky lumps. The big danger with squid is that, because it stays on forever and never breaks up, you can be tempted to leave the same piece on for hours on end. The same rules apply to squid as other species—fresh bait at every cast.

Fresh squid is hard to obtain in many parts of the country and you may have to make do with frozen packets but these seem to be very good.

SHRIMP

As I said earlier, shrimp as a bait is very localised in its use. The place where it scores time after time is alongside where shrimp boats sort out their catch and riddle out the undersize ones. Obviously, the fish here get used to feeding on shrimp and attack greedily any hook baited with them, but unless you know of such a place where experience has proved its worth I would advise you to treat it with caution.

To hook shrimp push the hook through the back two segments and put a couple of shrimps on at a time. It does not cast very well because of the softness of the bait so exercise care in casting.

The two kinds of shrimp used are raw or cooked. There does not seem to be much difference in effect between the two but raw shrimps would appear more natural. Getting fresh shrimps can be a problem, but if you live near a flat sandy beach you should be able to get enough to fish with by using a small meshed net a few feet across, pushed through the water at low tide. Alternatively, there may be a few professional shrimpers around who would part with a bagful for a few pence.

MUSSEL

This is a bait that I think has a bigger following than it deserves. On the East and North East coasts it is relied on far too much by anglers who use it, more because of its convenience than for its fish-catching capabilities. It certainly does catch fish but there are better baits in both winter and summer.

Two types of mussel are used—cooked or raw. Cooked mussels are an abomination and the last resort of an angler too lazy to shell raw ones. To get a mussel out of its shell take a sharp knife, split round the shell and break the seal. Then gradually work the knife blade across the inside of the shell cutting away the mussel from the roof of the shell until you can prise open the shell completely without breaking up the flesh. To get the flesh out of the bottom half of the shell, just scrape it out with a knife.

I tie mussel on the hook by taking about six and twisting them onto the shank of the hook round and round and finishing by pushing the hook point through the little black tongue. Then I take some mussel thread—or ordinary cotton—and twist it around the bait so that it binds the mussel to the hook. When it seems secure give the mussel a strong tug and just break it off. There is no need to finish off with a knot because that last strong tug to break the cotton bites into the flesh and holds the end of the thread. A point to watch when using mussel is that your hook does not get choked up with cotton. Clear the old cotton off every now and then.

This is one bait that I never gather fresh. The mussels that cling to my local pier and breakwaters are small and not much good at all. I buy mine by the quart, uncooked, from a shell fish shop.

UNUSUAL BAITS

Here I am listing the more unorthodox baits that do catch fish but for various reasons are not commonly used in match fishing.

Sandeel

A very good bait in a boat for pollack and cod and a good bass bait from the beach, but live sandeel is hard to cast a long way out. If I was fishing a match in one of the areas where they can be found naturally I think I would be very tempted to fish with a two hook trace, one hook with a live sandeel and the other with crab on, and try for bass.

Cockles and Whelks

If you are contemplating fishing a match and you have only cockles and whelks (or limpets)—do not bother.

Clams

Syphon clams make a conical depression in the sand and have a long feeder that sticks out of the shell. They can make good bait for bass, cod and, surprisingly, flatfish. They are a chancy bait and I would not go to a match with nothing else but clams, but if you find a few while digging worm then by all means try them as an alternative bait to crab or worm. Hook them on in the same way as mussels.

Hermit Crabs

These are very localised in their distribution but I have fished with them quite a lot in Scotland, where they abound naturally, and they fish very well. To collect them you can either use a drop net, with a piece of fish in it, over the end of a pier or jetty or wade around in the water at low tide and pick them. Hermit crabs live in disused whelk shells so just look inside the shell and, if you see some feelers and a big nipper, that is a hermit crab.

To get to the crab break the end off the shell with a rock or little hammer and expose the top half. Be careful not to crush the crab in your enthusiasm to break the shell, though! When you have broken off part of the shell you should be able to get a firm grip on the hermit and, by gently twisting and pulling, draw it out of the shell. To hook the hermit you need a fairly big hook—say, a 1/0 or possibly larger—and you push the point through the soft tail part and out through the front of the head. It stays on quite well this way and will withstand a powerful cast.

Any bait I have not described in this section is either very specialised in one particular area (kipper fillets outside a waterfront kipper factory) or it does not work well enough to be used with confidence in a match.

These eels have just won the author two more cups and first place in the loco open at Fleetwood.

The moment everyone is waiting for—the weighing in.

[3]

Bite Detection

Why, oh why, is this vitally important factor in fishing so often skimped in angling books. You can have the finest rod and reel in the world and the best bait but if you cannot recognise a bite you might as well not be there. It is not as straightforward as it seems, either. We have all had days when the rod has been bounced up and down on the rest or walked away for half an hour to return and find a fish on, but those days are few and far between and in match fishing you just cannot afford to trust to luck. Not only do different fish give different bites, but the same fish in a different environment gives a different bite. Founders that give timid tugs on a flat beach will often nearly bounce the rod into the water in an estuary. So, although there is nothing quite so unpredictable as fish (unless it is fishermen), in this chapter I will tell you how to recognise most kinds of bites and how to hit them.

FISHING WITH THE ROD IN THE REST

Strictly speaking you should have the rod in the rest as little as possible in a match because then you just cannot hope to hit lightning bites. Many species rarely give you a second chance to hook them, notably bass, and the bite you miss by having your rod in the rest could be the clincher.

However, there are times when you cannot avoid it—when you are rummaging in your tackle box or preparing bait or even munching sandwiches—so a knowledge of how to tell bites on the rest is useful.

The biggest headache when the rod is on the rest is in telling when it is the tide and current pulling at the tip and when it is a fish. To strike at every quiver and pull will hinder you in catching anything at all, and there are many times when you just cannot seem to make out what is causing the movement.

Firstly, think of the way a fish moves the rod when it bites. It usually takes the bait in its mouth in a big suck, which is what causes the conventional 'knock' we all know (or should know) so well. This sucking makes the rod dip *sharply* down and up. If the tackle were drifting along the bottom and was snagging as it rolled the action would be more smooth, showing as a long pull forwards and then a sharp jerk backwards. To get the hang of this action go and fish in an estuary when the tide is running hard and, if you cast in without any bait on, you will see the action on the rod tip caused by currents.

Incidentally, if your rod is standing in the water on the rest and there is anything like an edge on the water the rod will hammer wildly everytime a wave touches the butt, so do not be misled.

If you are fishing on a flat sandy beach where there is very little surf and very little current, put the rod on the rest so that it meets it at about the ferrule. On a normal beach rod this will mean that 6 feet of the rod is above and 6 feet below. The more distance there is between the tip and the rod rest the more sensitive the tip is to the terminal tackle, and any slight movement is immediately and clearly registered on the tip.

Because of the sensitivity, though, if the sea is running hard and you have such a distance as this between tip and rest you will find the tip is permanently waving about and it is impossible to tell a bite. Consequently, in surf or in choppy seas, make the distance between tip and rest much less so that wave bites are not so noticeable.

If you are on a steep beach, or one where there is a good surf running close in, those one piece rests that stick into the ground can be useful in clearing the first few rows of breakers.

Fishing in wind can be very frustraing. I do not mind rain but wind really upsets me in match fishing. The rod is continually waving around and only if forced to would I use a rest in windy weather. Holding either the rod or the line is a much more sensitive guide.

In windy conditions, instead of a rest I usually just prop the rod on my tackle box with the tip facing into the wind. By pointing the rod into the wind you get less disturbance from cross winds. As with fishing in heavy surf keep the distance between tip and rest fairly short.

Incidentally, when fishing on piers which have railings along them use exactly the same principles for rough and calm weather.

Bow-lining is a method of detection using the rest which can be extremely sensitive and effective. As the name implies it means using the natural bow that appears in the line when fishing in wind or heavy seas. There is an automatic tendency to keep tightening up the line whenever a bow appears in the belief that with a bow in the line all the power of a strike will be absorbed by the slack line and the hook will remain motionless. This is not strictly true; the line is up against considerable resistance from both the wind and the current and it takes a surprising amount of force for the line to cut through either the tide or the wind. It is far easier for the line to travel across the current than directly against it. An analogy is the man rowing a boat who finds he can travel quicker by tacking, which is going across the current, instead of directly against it.

So with fishing line: as you put the pressure on the line to pull it towards you it does not just straighten out against the pull but moves across and sinks home the hook in just the same way as if you were fishing with a tight line on a calm day.

To illustrate this more clearly just walk onto the beach on a windy day, cast out about fifty or sixty yards and let a bow appear in your line. Mark where the terminal tackle is on the beach, go back to your rod and strike it with the bow in. When you look at your tackle, you will find it has moved a fair distance in spite of the bow, proving that striking with a bow in the line *does* hook the fish.

If you want to cut down the amount of drag on the line from either the wind or a current then reduce the diameter of your line as much as you dare. The smaller the diameter of the line the less resistance it will offer to the current.

However, the important thing to remember in bow line bites is that they only work efficiently in strong current or wind. If fishing on a calm day, just let the line go slack and the force of the strike will be absorbed into the slack and the hook will remain motionless. Remember there must be a force pressing against the line to bow-line. The bites register on the tip in exactly the same way as if you were tight-line fishing in calm weather.

HOLDING THE ROD

This is the second best way I know of telling bites and it has the big advantage over the rod in a rest of giving you the chance to hit the fish at the first bite—very useful if the fish only intended biting once. You are in immediate contact with the fish and able to strike the moment it takes without the few seconds delay of seeing the bite, picking up the rod and striking that is caused when you use a rod rest.

Hold the rod in the way you prefer, or whichever way is more comfortable, but preferably at about 45 degrees in front of you. This gives the rod a bigger sweep when you strike.

You can either feel for the bites or the vibrations the bite causes or watch the tip to see the rod move. Either way you are in immediate contact with the fish. You *can* keep the rod on the rest and pick it up to feel for the second bite with the rod in your hand, but only if there *is* a second bite. It is far better to be in contact with the tackle all the time.

FINGERING FOR BITES

I had better not claim that I invented this way of detecting bites or someone will tell me they used it fifty years ago; but I had never seen it before and it is ruthlessly effective.

Basically you hold the line instead of the rod and can feel every movement the bait makes. The first tentative pluck that hardly moves the rod tip comes over loud and clear.

The first time I used the art of fingering for bites was about fifty miles from the sea when I was fishing for tench one night. I had forgotten my flashlight and was rather puzzled as to how I could tell the bites without anything to light up my swing tip. It was then that I hit on the idea of pointing the rod at the water, crooking the line around my finger and thumb and feeling for the bite.

It worked like a dream and I had one of the best night's tench fishing I have ever had. All I had on the line was a big shot squeezed on above my lobworm and every time a fish picked up the bait I could feel it.

It was coincidental, but the first time I thought of using fingering in the sea, was when I forgot my lamp one night and used the same principle of pointing the rod at the water and crooking the line around finger and thumb, I hardly missed a bite.

Obviously, the method is every bit as effective during the day too, and now almost without exception I finger for bites. You can very easily learn to differentiate between what is the current and wind and what is a fish.

Another advantage of fingering is that you can let your eyes, but not your attention, wander while you are holding the line. You can prop the rod on your rest while you are pointing it at the tackle so that there is no strain on your arms and you can keep it up quite easily all the way through a match.

NIGHT FISHING

Without hesitation, I would say finger for bites at night. As an alternative, you can hold the rod but putting it on a rest is not a good way at all. The light of a flickering torch or tilley lamp is a poor substitute for direct contact with the tackle.

If there is a bit of a wind the rod has a habit of vanishing from view and for a moment it looks as though you have had a bite. Also, if you are tired, your eyes can play strange tricks. But if you are holding line you can shut your eyes and still feel a bite the second it happens.

IN GENERAL

No matter what method you use to indicate the bite, striking at the right moment is important. I call it hitting a bite 'on the bounce' which is striking as the rod first begins a dip or on the first pluck in your fingers. Strike hard and strike firm. If the fish has run in with the bait and you have got a slack line, that is a slack-line bite and, to hit it, you have to run back fast up the beach, reeling in fast until the line arches into the fish.

There is a terrific amount of stretch in many lines and, when fishing at only moderate distances, you have to really punch the rod back to get the hook to move. At very long distances—over one hundred and fifty yards—you will hardly move the tackle at all and probably do little more than tighten up the line.

Remember speed is an important factor in hitting bites.

4

Tackle

As the correct bait is important in match fishing, so, too is the correct tackle. You have to be prepared for any situation that might crop up. It is no good going to a match with a couple of hooks and weights thrown in the bottom of a basket and hoping that you do not lose any tackle or have to make a sudden change of tactics because when the time comes that you want to do something different you will not be able to.

I have been accused of carrying excess equipment that I would never need except in very rare circumstances. That is probably true, because I am waiting for thos extraordinary circumstances to appear. When they do, everything I need will be at my fingertips.

Perhaps the best way of describing the equipment the matchman should possess is to list everything I consider necessary, and why.

Rods
Very much a personal thing, rods. I certainly have my preferences, not just for match fishing but for general sea fishing, but I would not say that rod design or make really matters, so long as it fulfills the two major requirements of any rod—casting and striking.

It is very much the vogue these days to have fast-taper rods that can punch a weight over 200 yards, and thousands of pounds have been spent on advertising to convince sea anglers that fast-taper rods are the cat's whiskers.

But I do not think that, as far as fishing goes, it makes much difference whether the rod is fast-taper, reverse-taper or just plain, ordinary, thick at one end and thin at the other, so long as it does the job properly.

The thing to avoid in buying a rod is too soft an action. If the whole rod is floppy much of the impact of a strike is taken out by the rod and the hook can remain motionless. Also avoid the rod that is like a broomstick and never bends at all. Its big disadvantage is that bite detection is hard because the tip will not move to indicate a bite.

The thing to do is to find one rod that suits you personally and stick with it. The rod I call my number one was bought secondhand a good many years ago and is still as efficient as when it was new. It has a new set of good rod rings put on it every Spring, the corks patched up and does everything I ask of it. For the record, it is a Martin James Keelson, but I think they are no longer made.

This model has the reel fitting fixed at the bottom of the butt instead of the top, so that the reel is controlled during casting by the hand at the bottom of the rod. This sometimes called the South African style and it is popular among some tournament casters, but I do not think the position of the reel makes any difference.

I have a second type of rod which I use occasionally for certain styles of fishing. It is a light, nine foot, hollow glass salmon spinning rod which is useful when fishing light in estuaries for flounders and eels.

A word on maintenance. Keep a regular check on the wear and tear on the rings. Many makes of ring are prone to grooving and these grooves will cut your line to ribbons if you let the line run through them. Keep the ferrule well oiled so that the two halves fit snugly and tightly and when they are pulled apart they 'plop'.

One bad practice I see occasionally is pushing the ferrules in only part way. This is caused either by the ferrule being a bad fit or an accumulation of dirt and grit on it. If you use a rod with the ferrule only half in you are asking for trouble. The strain on the ferrule will buckle it at the first big cast or big fish and you will be in trouble. If the ferrule does not fit then spend an evening with a strip of emery cloth and get it to fit.

In general then, find a rod that works and stick with it.

Reels

Up until a few years ago the multiplier market was completely dominated by the Americans. There were a few European beach casting multipliers made, but in the main they were not worth the boxes they were packed in.

However, all that is over now and the competition gets fiercer and fiercer in the reel game. British, French and Swedish firms are all producing quality gear that is on a par and sometimes superior to their American opposites numbers.

On the choice of reel, I must firstly say get a multiplier and learn how to use it. I know there are plenty of supporters of fixed spool and wooden 'Scarborough' reels but they have only limited use so far as I am concerned. Fixed-spool reels are not too bad for casting if you know how to handle one properly but they fall down badly on reeling in. Get a big weight on the end of the line, either fish or weeds, and the job of reeling in becomes agony. It is very often the case that sea anglers who use fixed spool reels began their fishing career in freshwater where fixed-spool reels are ideal. When they turn to the sea, they find multipliers difficult to master and take the easy way out by buying a fixed-spool reel. Using a fixed-spool reel in the sea may be easy but it is not efficient, and what we want in a match is efficiency.

So if you are one of the fixed-spool men my advice is to get a good multiplier, lots of line and weights go to a quiet beach and practise.

Those big 'Scarborough' wooden centre-pins are horrible and grossly inefficient. About the only place where they are still used with any regularity now is on the North East coast, but I am glad to see that the trend is towards multipliers. If you possess one of these Scarborough reels, then I suggest you burn it.

Side-cast reels are one stage better than fixed-spool reels because they work well under strain and cast quite well, but they are a clumsy looking thing and I certainly would never use one.

I hope I have convined everyone to use only multipliers for competitive fishing and I will now describe the best types of multiplier to use.

No serious minded match angler should go near the water's edge without at least two multipliers, and I usually take three.

You need one for the general run-of-the-mill fishing that has a good line capacity (at least 250 yards), a good rate of retrieve and casting ability. In this class I put the Penn Surfmaster 200, Penn Squidder, Intrepid Fastbacks, Pirates and Buccaneers, Mitchell 600 and Abu 9000.

I have possessed all of these reels at one time or another and would feel happy with any one of them. Without doubt the Abu 9000 is the best of the lot, but then at the price you would expect it to be!

I have, as reserve to my 9000, a Squidder which is a functional reel that works well, although the spools are apt to crack under stress. The reserve reel is there in case of a break down of the first reel or the loss of line. If you have a reel with a plastic spool then carry a spare spool of line with you.

The other type of reel that it is useful to have with you is a narrow spool reel for distance casting. I take it that the reader is familiar with the fact that light, narrow spool reels do cast much further when loaded with a light line and leader, and if you are fishing a spot where the fish are a long way out a distance reel can be invaluable. In this class I put the Penn Surfmaster 100, the Abu 7000 and 6000C and the Mitchell 602AP. I have used all of these reels at one time or another and they are all about as good as each other except that the 6000C has a lower line capacity and retrieve rate than I would have liked.

If, through finance or other reasons, you have to manage with one reel then pick a good one from the list of bigger line capacity reels I have mentioned and get a spare spool for it. If you think your budget will stand two reels then go for one of the narrow spool reels and if you are really on a spending spree then get another big line capacity reel as a spare.

I also have a fourth reel lying in wait at home—a freshwater fixed-spool reel loaded with 9 lb line. I only take this fishing if I can reasonably expect that I might be tempted to spin for either bass, mackerel or coalfish and, of course, I use it with the salmon spinning rod I mentioned earlier.

Do keep all your reels in good order and well oiled and in a bag or a box that will keep the sand and sea out. If you leave them lying in the bottom of the basket with no protection you are just asking for trouble.

Lines

Lines can make all the difference between success and failure in fishing. If you have a cheap line you are making a false economy because with fishing lines—like most other things in fishing—you get exactly what you pay for.

Quite obviously monofilament is the only line to use from the beach, but there are varying types of mono on the market. Basically, it falls into two categories—pre-stretched and un-stretched. Pre-stretched lines have much of the natural stretching taken out of them and so, when you strike with a pre-stretched line, you have a better degree of impact with the tackle.

Unstretched lines tend to vary in quality from mediocre to down-right abominable and, as I have said, price is the indication of quality. Get a good line and it will last a season and retain much of its original suppleness and strength. Get a bad line and you will find that after a few weeks, you are getting bunching on the reel and finding it twisted and frayed.

Ideally, I suppose, the very latest non-stretch line that has hit the market would be ideal, but it is very expensive and if you are fishing regularly in a place that is snaggy it is going to run out very expensive over the year.

The breaking strain is largely dependent on the weight you are casting with not, as is commonly believed, the type of bottom you are fishing over. If you cast with a six ounce weight then about 27 lb breaking strain is ideal and if you use a four ounce weight, then go for something about 24 lb.

In picking the breaking strain of line for a reel, what you should be striving for is the minimum practical size. The less the breaking strain of the line the less the diameter and the less the diameter the better the line will cast.

The choice should be strong enough to withstand the shock of an occasional bunch-up yet not be so heavy that it cuts down your casting distances. That is why for my general purpose reels I load with 27 lb line.

I do not agree with the idea of some anglers on the North East coast that where you are fishing on rough kelpy ground you should scale up to something around 40 lb breaking strain. I have fished most places on the East coast and I firmly believe that once you get stuck into a lump of kelp a ship's anchor rope would not pull you free.

For your small spool-reel you want a line around 20 lb breaking strain with a heavy leader of something around 30 lb for the first few yards of the reel to take the shock of the cast. The idea of having a thinner diameter line backed by a leader is that as the line diameter diminishes so the casting range of the reel increases. So, bearing in mind that the whole idea of having a narrow spool-reel is to get maximum casting distances, the thinner the main line the further it will cast. However, if you drop the main line too drastically (say, down to 12 lb breaking strain), you will find that although you are casting further you are snapping the line at every bird's nest or bunch.

On maintenance of fishing lines, keep trimming a few yards off the end about once a week, or more often if you are fishing over rough ground, as the strain of casting and the wear of being pulled over rough, rocky or musselly ground can weaken the line so much that you will begin to get mysterious snappings of the line on casting. Renew the line about once a year and try to avoid getting knots in it. This often causes bunching. A good idea is to reverse the line halfway through the year so that the line that is never used replaces the end that takes all the strain.

A golden rule you should never break is to keep the spools full on all your reels and never let them get low. If you do, you could well find that on long casts you will be running out of line.

Hooks

The fishing tackle market seems to be singularly lacking in good fishing hooks. This is the plea of just about every angling writer these days, yet manufacturers seem reluctant to produce an expensive hook. I have tried just about every type of hook on the market at one time or another and not one has really satisfied me one hundred per cent. I am reasonably happy these days with the fine wire hooks that are imported from France which have good hooking power, hold a bait well and are quite strong in the bigger sizes. In the smaller sizes they fall down badly, on strength and bend very easily.

The fault of most hooks is in the basic design. If a hook is blunt—as is usual—you can sharpen it, but you cannot very well re-make it. Points to avoid in a hook are too big a barb and incorrect temper.

If the barb is too pronounced it will have a tendency to rip soft baits as you push them on the hook and will present a bigger resistance to a fish when striking. However, lately I have been modifying the barbs on my hooks by nipping them further in towards the shank with a small pair of pliers. You have to be careful not to damage the point in doing this and you may well find that a good number of the hooks lose their barbs in this operation. This is fine because it is showing up those hooks that have the wrong temper before they are used.

The best angle to close them up to is rather difficult to define, but I have been fishing with some where the barb is nearly on top of the shank and they have still caught fish.

Your catches of flatfish will certainly benefit from a smaller barb because these are a fish that so often hook themselves. Quite obviously, it's easier for them to get fast on a hook that slides easily into the flesh than on one that presents a lot of resistance and, in spite of what some may think, fish can't get off small barb hooks any easier than big barbed hooks.

When you buy your hooks it's best to do so in quantities of a hundred, because you can safely bet that they are all the same temper in the same box. To test hooks before you buy them take three out of a box and, holding the shank in one hand, try to prise point apart with your fingers. If it moves easily the temper is too soft, if it snaps it is too brittle. If the hooks are only small, say size 4, then even on the finest hook made will bend, but you shouldn't be able to do it easily. On anything larger than a size 1 you shouldn't be able to budge it. Always test three of the hooks because you may have picked up the only bad hook in an otherwise good packet or, conversely, the only good hook in a bad packet.

You don't have to buy many hooks to realise that different firms have a different interpretation of the seemingly standard sizes. A No. 1 hook in the eyes of one manufacturer can be vastly different from another's, so rather than blindly ask for a size you think is right have a good look at the hooks in the shop first and check that they look the right size for the job in mind.

Hook styles to definitely avoid in match fishing are the japanned black salmon low water hooks which are immensely strong but are too thick in the wire and have too large a barb for practical fishing with softer baits such as crab, which they tend to rip up.

Another ghastly type are those beak hooks with a couple of bait-holding barbs on the shank. Again, these barbs tend to rip the bait rather than help to keep it on.

As I said, I personally use nothing but fine wire hooks, but everyone to their choice.

On maintenance, I would say that no matter what the quality of a hook it should be thrown away after every fishing trip and replaced. Keep the points sharp with a handy stone or file. I have a little warding file in my basket which does the job admirably but a piece of fine emery cloth stuck on a little piece of wood would do fine. One little tip I sometimes employ is to stick a strip of emery cloth on the cork handle of the rod so that it is easy to sharpen up hooks at every cast.

Needless to say you should have a complete range of hooks in every size from No. 6 to 5/0 and they must be kept in a dry place safe from rust. If you are fishing over rough stone ground check the hooks regularly to see that none have been bent over on rocks.

Weights

The style and weight of leads is very much a personal thing. For my part, there are only two weights I use with any regularity—five ounce bombs and six ounce anchors. I have a mould for each and cast my own as and when I need them. If you do not fancy the bomb shape then the streamlined torpedo shape is probably just as effective for casting.

The only time I use an anchor is in rough weather or when the tide race is too fierce for an ordinary weight to hold. I do not use the type of anchor you buy in the shop. though, Mine, being home made, have prongs on them of about four inches and hold firm even in the stiffest of tide races. They are made in a softish wire so that should they get stuck round an obstacle they will pull out easily.

If you prefer a lighter weight then the two weights you should stick with are a four ounce torpedo and a four ounce anchor.

Weights to definitely avoid are those club shaped star weights that look like some mediaeval war weapon. They do not hold bottom well and are about as streamlined in the air as a fat pig. Grip weights (those round, studded weights, flat with a hole in the middle) are another type that does not cast well.

Obviously there is no maintenance involved in keeping up your stock of weights but always allow for a few breakages when you go to a match and take plenty of weights with you. Nothing could be worse than having to pack up because you have run out of leads.

Basket or Box?

Not many years ago, nobody thought of carrying their tackle in anything other than a basket but in recent years the use of canvas, plastic and rigid boxes has grown. Of these, I prefer a watertight box because the inside of a wicker basket is perpetually getting damp and rusting everything. Rain often trickles down into a basket and, again, dampens everything.

About the best tackle box on the market now is one that has a liftout section of plastic compartments for hooks, swivels, split rings and the like. It incorporates a seat and is big enough even for the vast amount of tackle I take down on the beach.

Equally suitable are the cantilever boxes which open to reveal dozens of trays full of all your tackle. The drawback to these is that they are usually too small to carry everything but if you get a smallish cantilever box it will fit snugly inside a basket or big box.

I might add that a very useful item in match fishing is a canvas shoulder bag that can be slung round the neck and carried all day long. These are very useful if you are fishing a spot where there is a very flat beach and you are continually backing up.

What odds and ends should you carry in your tackle box? Certainly a good selection of link swivels, ordinary swivels, three-way swivels and split rings. These are all necessary for making up traces and you should never be without them.

A sharp knife is necessary for all the many cutting jobs you do during the course of a match and if you are using crab, include a small flat board about nine inches square for cutting it on.

Carry a spare length of line for tying traces. I keep mine on an old spool that fishing line is supplied on. But do not fall into the trap of using up old worn out line for this purpose or something that has been bought very cheap. If you do, you could well find that the trace or hook snood is the weak link in the chain.

For keeping fish in, I always carry a couple of big strong plastic bags wrapped up together with an elastic band. A good dodge when you catch eels, which tend to keep wriggling out of the bag every few minutes, is to carry a clothes peg with you and peg up the top of the plastic bag to stop the fish getting out. Another peg on the end of your crab bag will stop them getting out, too. A word on keeping fish in plastic bags: watch out when fishing in hot sunny weather when great heat is generated inside a plastic bag if it is exposed to the sun. I once saw a fine catch of flounders literally fry inside a plastic bag on a summer's day and when the poor chap tipped his fish into the scales what fell out of his plastic bag was a mass of white cooked flesh and bones.

If you are using a plastic bag in summer then keep flushing the bag with cold sea water and keep it out of the sun.

Always kicking around at the bottom of my box are a couple of bottle corks. I have never used them, but I know of a situation where I might well need them. Not very long ago a good friend was fishing a club match on a beach that seemed to be alive with big crabs that were attacking the bait as soon as it hit the bottom. He combatted this by tying a couple of corks on his line just above the hooks and making the baits dance up from the bottom. After a while the crabs still took his bait but it took them much longer to get to it and, in the meantime, he caught two good flounders. One day I shall meet these same circumstances in a match and I will be ready.

I have a plastic wallet, normally used for carrying fly casts, which is ideal for made-up traces less the weight. It only cost me about 30p and is invaluable. A simple and cheap way of carrying traces is to put them (again minus the weight), in envelopes, seal them and write on the front what they contain.

I have a set of mackerel feathers with me at all times. A few matches, where mackerel are not commonly caught, allow you to fish for mackerel with feathers (three hooks only, of course) and you could easily pull off an angling coup by spending the whole match feathering. You will probably get some mumbling from other competitors who have not caught anything but you can laugh all the way to the prize table.

A little file or oilstone is essential. Hooks are blunt when you buy them and do not get any better for being knocked about in a tin. A good way of keeping hooks sharp during fishing is to sharpen all your hooks at home and then stick them between two strips of sticky tape to protect the points. As I said, in the section on hooks, you should check throughout the match that your hooks are sharp.

Always make sure you have a fish measure in your basket and check all the sizes of your fish if you are not sure of them. Many organisers have different lengths for fish that are unspecified by the

Ministry of Agriculture and Fisheries. Popular unspecified fish are bass, eels, flounders and tope. The bass minimum size varies from area to area but flounders and eels are more standard, being either eight or nine inches for flounders and anything up to twelve inches for eels.

You could run the risk of being disqualified if you go to the scales with undersize fish in some contests and, indeed, I remember not very long ago the chairman of the organising club being disqualified by his own committee for this offence. So obviously check all your own fish before you go to the scales. If you are in doubt about a fish and you think the officials are pretty keen on disqualification for undersize fish, it might be a good idea to approach one of the head marshals and ask for his help BEFORE you go near the scales. That way if there is any dispute at the weigh-in you have some support to fall back on.

I always carry a little spring balance with me for weighing my own catch as I go along. It's only curiosity, I suppose, but I like to know how things are going. If you are just fishing a club match and you are worried about a mate's increasing weight you can always offer to tell him what weight he has got so far!

I also have lying somewhere at the bottom of my box a ball point pen which is useful for stewards who have not got one. It is surprising how many stewards in a match lose or do not possess a pen to register your fish as being caught and, remember, it is *your* responsibility to see that every fish you catch is correctly booked down.

Lamps are obviously only used during night matches and, if it is an all-nighter, I like to have two lamps with me. Firstly a paraffin pressure lamp to generally brighten up the area, so that you can see where everything is, and a bicycle lamp (which I have slung round my neck). The lamp is tied onto a piece of ribbon and hangs about a foot below my chin. The advantage of this is that as you are reeling in it shines down on the spool giving you sufficient light to wind the line on evenly; and secondly, whenever you lean down to look in your box the lamp will shine into your box without you having to hold it. If you fish at night by having the rod on a rest, you can hold the bike lamp with one hand and direct it at the tip.

Wire traces are something you may need only very rarely when fishing for rays and conger but I always have a couple made up with big hooks in my trace wallet. You never need them but if you do you know they are there.

Spinners are something I have only ever used once in a match and then with only limited success. However, I always believe in allowing for the unexpected and there is always a toby lure in my basket.

I would never go anywhere without a few stainless steel paternosters. I know many anglers will think it strange that I should advocate using these mechanical things but, believe me, there are times when they are unbeatable for catching flatfish. However, the paternosters in my baskets are modified versions of what you see in the shops; the distance between the top boom and the bottom booms seems to get shorter and shorter. I cut through the swivel that is between the top and bottom booms and tie about a foot of very heavy line between the two. This gives a much better 'pat' that is less likely to tangle.

Never buy brass paternosters which go brittle and break and usually have only short booms. Go for stainless steel ones with three long booms. The main object of fishing with a paternoster is for flatfish and so I usually have them all ready made up with hooks on before I leave home. I always carry four with me on every trip with size 1 and 2 hooks on. To stop the hooks getting tangled up in everything else, I wrap them separately in newspaper and slip a rubber band around them. When you are making snoods for paternosters make sure that the length of the snood does not exceed the length of the boom. That way you will get less tangles of the snood wrapping round the wires.

Another very handy piece of equipment is a french boom. Often when fishing for cod with just one hook I use a french boom to keep the snood free from the main line and I do not think that it cuts down casting all that drastically. I prefer short french booms

about three inches long rather than the more common ones which are
about six or seven inches long, but they are not easy to obtain in
my area and I often make them myself from stainless steel wire.

Waders

Every serious match angler should have two pairs of waders.
A pair of the more common thigh waders whose uses everyone
knows, and a pair of breast-high waders or 'bellies' as they are often
called. Belly waders are more often associated with salmon fishing
but they can be used with devastating effect in the sea, too. Match
venues suitable for using 'bellies' are those on flat sandy beaches
where, at low water, the tide goes out for miles. On these beaches,
where the matches are usually fished on the flood, you can get a
tremendous advantage by being able to wade out further than most
anglers are casting. The cost of 'bellies' is not as prohibitive as you
might think, either. Although my pair cost something around
£10, when new, you can buy a pair in plastic from as little as
£1.75. Nearly all 'bellies' need a pair of shoes over them and I
use the feet cut from a pair of old waders.

5

Terminal Tackle

The terminal tackle is every bit as important as the bait itself because if a bait is incorrectly presented then it might as well not be presented at all. Judging by the weird and wonderful types of traces I have seen from time to time a chapter on making up successful traces would not come amiss.

The type of trace I use most often nowadays is the three hook trace. To make it you need: two big link swivels, two big three-way swivels, one split ring, one ordinary swivel, three hooks and a weight.

Start by attaching a link swivel to a three-way swivel by means of the split ring. Tie about 14 inches of line onto the bottom eye of the three-way and then attach another three-way swivel to it. Tie on another 14 inches of line to the bottom of the second three-way and slip the other link swivel onto this by means of the eye and then tie on the last single swivel.

Make two hook snoods of 10 inches and tie one onto each of the eyes that jut out from the three-way swivels. Make a third snood about 18 inches long and tie onto the bottom eye of the single swivel at the bottom of the trace. Your weight clips onto the sliding link swivel and the trace is made.

The link swivel at the end is for quick changing and you need to have a loop tied in the end of your reel line for this.

When fishing over rocky or weedy ground I still use one of these traces but take off the bottom trailing hook so that it doesn't get caught up and snag the whole trace.

It is not a cheap way of making a trace but it is a good one and all those swivels mean that should you get fish like eels that spin a lot in the water they have less chance of twisting all your tackle.

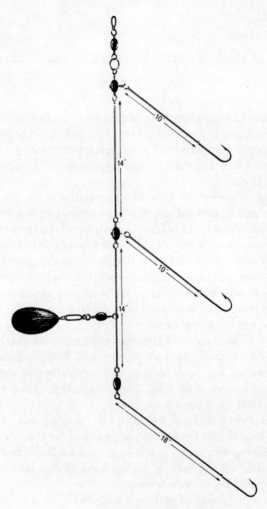

Three-hook Trace

To make a two-hook trace, simply leave out the second three-way swivel and just have one hook at the bottom and one above the weight—'one up and one down' as I call it. However, I am using the two-hook trace much less these days and preferring the three-hook trace as it gives me a chance of presenting a variety of bait to the fish. Even when fishing an exclusive crab spot with crab on all three hooks, I prefer the three-hook trace because it has more baits in the water and therefore has more smell.

I keep several traces made up in different hook sizes in my cast wallet and they keep flat because of not having a weight fixed on them.

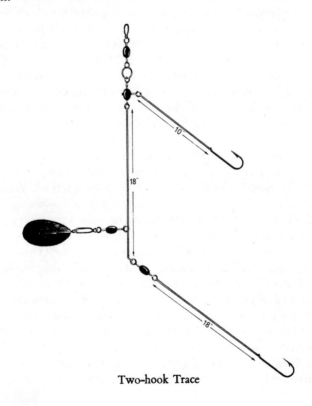

Two-hook Trace

Sometimes when the quarry is cod they lie a good way off the shoreline and the further the cast, the better. In circumstances like this I invariably go for a one hook trace with a french boom. This is simply a french boom with a snood and hook about eight inches fastened on the line about eighteen inches to two feet above the weight. With a narrow spool reel and a good cast I get good distances with this tackle. If you are not familiar with french booms, to attach them you simply twist the main line round and round the long side of the triangle and through the loop that they usually have and keep on doing so until the boom won't slide down the line.

The other terminal tackle I use is a paternoster as described in the previous chapter. The one point I would stress is to keep to the three-boom stainless steel variety and not brass or celluloid.

Occasionally you may have to use a wire trace when fishing for thornbacks and conger and the best way I think of fishing for these fish is to use a two-hook trace with a small bait such as worm or crab on the top hook and a two foot wire trace on the bottom with a big hook and a piece of mackerel on the wire trace. On wire traces I use Berkeley nylon covered wire and the Berkeley pincers and steel sleeves for fastening the wire to the hook. I find 35 lb breaking strain wire suitable for most kinds of fishing. If you have never had much experience of making up wire traces then I suggest you buy yourself a Berkeley set and get some practice. You can make wire traces at a fraction of the cost of shop-bought ones which often have cheap swivels that do not look very strong.

Very early on in this book I talked about the worm stop knot and how it could be used to keep big worms up the line and halt the tendency to fall into a lump around the shank of the hook. To make a worm stop knot tie your hook on in the normal way but leave a long length of line over after you have finished the knot and pulled it tight. Take this loose end and hold it alongside the main line and tie with the two lengths a couple or three overhand knots about an inch above the hook. When the bulbous knot is big enough, just tighten it and trim it in the normal way. This can be very effective for holding up big worms and is very simple to do.

Two Patting

This is a slang term for having two sets of tackle set up at the same time and is very good for saving time when the fish are biting well. All you do is to have at the end of your trace some means of detaching it quickly—either a link swivel or a spiral swivel—and have an identical set of tackle ready baited up on the beach so that, as soon as you bring in your set of tackle with fish on or in need of rebaiting, you simply twist off the one set of tackle and clip on the new. Cast out and then attend to the tackle with the fish on. This way you get maximum fishing time.

If you are using a stainless steel paternoster the job is just that bit easier because it will have a spiral built in for quick take off.

This method sounds very simple and efficient but for some reason the N.F.S.A. have seen fit to ban it. So if you are fishing in an N.F.S.A. organised match or one being fished to N.F.S.A. rules, do not use it.

6

Fishing Practice

Having got the right tackle and the right bait the next thing in match fishing is to have the right approach. The methods that will catch fish on a flat sandy beach may be next to useless on kelp infested rock edges, and tactics for a pier may be useless on a storm beach.

For this reason I am going to spend this chapter discussing some of the different techniques the successful matchman needs to apply when fishing on these contrasting grounds.

Estuaries

This is the hardest type of match fishing but also, I think, the most interesting. In most estuaries of any size you get all sorts of different varieties swimming up and down, hunting for the constant flow of food being washed down the river. Because the fishing is so varied it is difficult to know which fish to go for and where they will be lying, because the rules that apply to fish in the open sea do not apply in a river mouth. If anything, the fish behave more like the coarse fish further upstream than anything else, and it is in this manner that you have to think when figuring out where to cast.

Certainly it is a waste of time chucking and chancing in estuary fishing because it is a good bet that someone in the match knows a bit about rivercraft and is using it. The estuary goes through three stages—the flood tide, high water when the water stays still, and the ebb when it again rushes out with force.

Rule number one of estuary fishing is that fish do not like strong runs. You may find that a few bass like it rough but the type of fish that are interesting the match angler—flatties, eels and codling— steer clear when the tide runs hard. The reasons they move out of the main run of the river are: firstly, because it requires much less effort to keep their place in the water in a quieter current, and secondly, that the food being washed with the current has a tendency to be washed to the edges of the current where the rough meets the smooth.

When the tide is running hard in an estuary, finding this area of slacker water can really pay off and you can hit the fish when others are not holding bottom with the heaviest of leads. To spot these quieter waters look at the surface if the water is calm. You see tell-tale swirls where two currents of different speeds are meeting. It it is windy, watch out for debris being washed along with the force of the current. You will see some pieces going round in circles for a while before disappearing. It is in these circles that not only the surface rubbish, but the underwater rubbish will be congregating and, with it, the fish.

Where this area of slacker water is depends on the individual features of the river so there are no hard and fast rules, but after a couple of visits you should get to know the estuary in most of its moods. Do not be surprised when the tide is in full flood to find the fish only a matter of feet from the edge of the bank.

Just how far in some fish will lie in flood conditions was clearly illustrated to me a couple of years ago when I was going for a midweek preview to an estuary where our club was holding a match the following Sunday. More for the company than anything else I took along my Father who, incidentally, had never held a rod before in his life. Needless to say he found great difficulty in casting with the multiplier I had given him and his first cast ended up with the top boom of his stainless steel paternoster sticking out of the water and the bottom two hooks just lying submerged in the muddy estuary water. A few minutes elapsed while I untangled the ferocious mess and then I lifted the rod to bring the tackle out of the water. Imagine my absolute surprise when, although the top hook had been clear of the water, I found a decent sized flounder on the bottom hook!

I am not suggesting fishing close in to this extent all the time, but it does show you how close in the fish can sometimes be. When the river is in flood with the tide ripping through it is quite likely that you will find fish within six or twelve feet of the side and whenever I come across a match venue with these kind of conditions I always start fishing about eight feet out from the side. You can cast progressively a few feet further out each time till you either meet the real force of the tide or catch a fish. If you reach the full force then come back in again and repeat the process. If you catch a fish very close in then repeat the distance because it is likely that there will be a few more there, too.

When the tide stands still, either through dead high water or dead low water the pattern changes. The water near the edges tends to go completely dead with no movement in it at all and it is then that you have to cast far out to find the fish.

Although I said earlier that fish generally do not like the fierce run, they do like some movement in the water and will also keep in a moderate current. This current will be washing food along, which is something you would not get in a dead backwater. In an estuary it is general to find that the current from the actual river is somewhere in the middle but, obviously, if you are fishing in an estuary like the Bristol Channel, which is miles wide, you could not really hope to cast to the middle. But what you can do is to find water far out that has some run in it. You can spot it either by watching for the swirls of water or the bits of debris riding with the current.

To sum up then, the general rule is to cast short on the flood or the ebb and cast far at slack water. But do not hold to this as a hard and fast rule—there are occasions when fish do the strangest of things and if in a flood tide you find nothing anywhere close in then put on your heaviest anchor and belt it out for a try.

In estuary fishing as in all kinds of sea fishing do not fall into the depth trap—believing that you have got to have a good depth to catch fish. This is nonsense—you can catch fish in inches of water. I did just that and won an open with it. The match was being fished in the River Wyre estuary at Fleetwood and the catch was mainly eels. About half way through the match there were four of us, all with five fish taken early in the match when the tide had been at dead low. As soon as the full force of the incoming tide began to belt up the river the fish just went completely off the feed and seemed to vanish. I picked a small bootlace eel up about twelve feet out but there was still no sign of anything good enough to clinch the match.

The match was a rover—you could fish where you wanted—and it was then that I decided to take a gamble and moved off upstream into a backwater—a tiny branch of the river where there was no current at all. There was no water in it as the tide had only just began to flood it but I decided there might be a chance of a bootlace or two about, fish too small to withstand the force of the current. I scaled the tackle down to size four hooks and put on a two ounce lead, more than sufficient for this short stretch of muddy water which was not more than twenty feet across. I baited up with crab again and, lobbing the tackle in, held the rod in my hands and tightened up the line. I got the shock of my life when as I tightened up the line the top swivel poked out of the water. I must have been fishing in only inches of water! But before I had a chance to regret the cast the rod jerked violently in my hands and I instinctively struck into what proved to be the biggest eel of the day—just over one pound.

As soon as I had swung in the fish and changed to a fresh baited trace I cast to the exact spot again but by now the tide had made a little and the top swivel stayed submerged. Within a minute I had another eel on the bank (or should I say the mud) and in the half hour remaining of the match that I fished in this tiny spot, I took four good eels and a flounder.

At the weigh-in I learned that after I had left there had been no more fish from the main river and I won the match with over 3 lb to spare.

I do not think this idea would have worked for every specie of fish, certainly unlikely for fish such as codling and whiting. But for flatfish and eels watch out for a backwater and earmark it for use when the tide begins to rush.

Fishing on Flat Sand

This is the kind of match fishing I have been brought up on and I reckon to do fairly well at it. The most important thing to realise is that different fish lie in different depths and consequently at different distances out. Of the common fish found on sandy beaches the following may be said to be generally true: flounders and eels will lie in the first forty or fifty yards from the shore line. They may be as close in as ten yards, which is why you so often see young lads who cannot cast or older anglers who get buch-ups and fall short catching the odd eel and flounder, especially on the flood tide when these two fish follow the tide in very closely.

Believe it or not, the biggest obstacle in catching fish close in on a beach is having the ability to cast short distances. This might sound crazy but there are many anglers who just have to hurl the tackle out as far as they can at every throw. I blame the advent of compound taper rods for this with their accent on distance, distance, distance. Every week when you pick up an angling paper, you see full colour advertisements preaching the gospel of distance until it has become a mark of angling competency to cast rather than to catch fish.

So, if you can cast short and feel confident, you are well on the way to being a successful flounder angler. The end tackle for sandy beaches where there are no snags is invariably either a trace or a stainless steel paternoster. If you think that the flounders and eels are not there—as they sometimes are not in winter—and you want to try for dabs, whiting or codling then you are quite in order to try distance casting, in fact the further the better with these three fish in daylight. It is here that belly waders come into their own and I know of many matches that have been won by using them.

If the beach is especially flat and therefore you can wade a long way out, you do not want to return to the shore at every cast, wasting valuable fish time. It is a far better proposition to pack all the essential gear you are likely to need (which will be a spare set of tackle, bait and fish bag), into a haversack which can be slung round your neck allowing you to stand out in the water for long spells. If you are doing this then a tripod rod rest, which will support itself, is invaluable both for propping the rod on while you are busy and for holding spare sets of baited up tackle.

However, the decision of where to fish in the summer on a flat beach can be tricky. You could catch flounders close in, and dabs—and possibly plaice—further out. What you have to do in this case is to try and figure out where you think the biggest bulk of fish would come from. Remember that it could take three dabs to make up the weight of one good flounder, but could you catch enough flounders close in? The question is really best answered by personal knowledge of the beach or by trial and error on the day.

Every flat beach has its hot spots no matter if the quarry is flounders or dabs. There are certain types of bottom and contours of the sand that attract many types of fish and spotting these as you back up with the tide and making use of them can often pick up a few fish for you. Most sandy beaches have gulleys on them, usually in parallel to the shoreline and through these gulleys the first rush of water comes on the flood. When the tide moves in to completely flood all the beach, there will still be a current in these gulleys and the current will be collecting food there. Consequently, fish should be gathering there also. Watch for these gulleys and small dips in the sand before you take up your place on the beach so that you will have a couple to fish in when the tide reaches high water.

Similarly, look out for little stony outcrops or pebbles in a small patch where all kinds of fish will root about once the tide has covered them. Equally good are breakwaters which always have a current washing up against them creating a turbulence that attracts fish. But make sure you get the right side of a breakwater so that the tide is not always washing your tackle into the woodwork.

But perhaps the best feature of all I look for on a beach is a sewer pipe. It is a fact that all kinds of delectable and palatable forms of fish food wash down household sewers and most forms of fish like them. I don't think I need to point out, however, that sewers from chemical or mining sources are not good fishing spots but death traps for marine life.

One of the principle reasons that you get such a concentration of fish round a pipe is that the smaller marine creatures such as shrimps and crabs congregate there, too. Even if the pipe is a small one with only a trickle coming out of it it is still worth trying.

Watch for the film of scum on the surface that comes from sewers. It will always leave a tell-tale trail and be running with the current. Cast into the middle of this trail or, if you can, right in front of the sewer itself and you shouldn't come unstuck.

As the quarry is very often flatfish on sandy beaches a bit of slow retrieving doesn't come amiss now and again. I don't have the absolute faith in this that some anglers seem to, but sometimes it can pay dividends to give the bait a move. If nothing else you are covering more ground than the angler with a static bait.

Very often the tide has a long way to travel to the high water mark on flat sandy beaches and when fishing on the flood you are continually being driven backwards. You can make use of this by using your high capacity multiplier and belly waders and by leaving the tackle about three hundred yards out before you run out of line and have to bring it in.

Fishing in Surf

Surf beaches, where the shoreline shelves steeply and the wind and tide often whips the water up into a heavy surf, are not my favourite type of match venue. Firstly because, in match conditions, they are not usually very productive and tend to be won with just a few small fish or one big bass.

In most parts of Great Britain, with the exception of much of the East coast, bass are usually the summer quarry on these types of beach, with a few eels and flounders thrown in for good measure.

Consequently, to stand any chance of winning this type of summer match, you have to fish for bass rather than try to pick up the odd small fish or two.

On bass the only thing I can say is to be ready for the first bite and hit that first bite as soon as you can, because you won't get a second chance. This business of second or third breaker out to catch bass is all rubbish. If I could predict where the bass will be as easily as that I would win every bass match I entered. It is true to say that, in general, ALL the fish lie fairly close in on steep surf beaches. This is because the rolling action of the surf keeps a constant motion in the water, stirring up the bottom and disturbing buried food. For this reason I very rarely cast great distances on this type of beach but keep well inshore to where I think the most turbulence is likely to be.

Again, on a surf beach it can be invaluable to have a pre-match look at the beach at low water to see the type of ground you will be fishing over. If you have any choice in the matter at all, try and find some beach with some character about it.

Fishing on Rock Edges

This mode of match fishing is largely restricted to the East and North East coasts of England and parts of Scotland. To anyone not used to it it can be very frustrating. All the normal rules of fishing do not apply on rock edges and you need a completely different approach to it. Usually, you can forget casting for two reasons: one, the fish will be lying close in because of the depth you get inshore, and two, because where there are rock edges there is usually kelp and if you get a fish on and try to bring it in through weed you will not only lose the fish but all your tackle too.

On this kind of fishing, which is usually exclusively cod fishing, I adopt a one hook tackle with the weight at the bottom so that there are no trailing hooks to catch on waving bushes. I know that the general view on the East coast is to fish with a 'rotten bottom', which is using a length of line for attaching the weight of a much weaker strength than the rest of the line so that, the theory goes, when you get snagged up with a fish on all you lose is your weight and not the fish.

I never use such a set-up because I have never had need to. We all accept that a knot is the weakest link in the line so that if you are using the trace with a french boom on as I described earlier, the only knot in the line is just above the weight and that is where the line should part if you are using good line. But I do recommend the 'rotten bottom' method if you are losing a lot of tackle.

Finding a spot to fish on rock edges is very much a matter of local knowledge, which is why in East coast roving matches fished on the rocks, only, the locals ever win. They have the local knowledge to know the hot spots at the current time. It would be a different story if, as in most other matches, you had to draw for a place. All you can really rely on, when picking your fishing spot, is local know-ledge and the accuracy of comment from the match organisers, who usually do their best to tell you the good spots.

If you are new to this type of fishing then, in general, I would say that most of the best weights come from the rock edges and not the clear sand beaches you find in the East and which look so easy to fish.

Pier Fishing

In general, pier matches tend to be rather a lucky dip. You find that most of the fish are at the end and that whoever draws the point of the pier or breakwater usually wins. There are a few exceptions where the winner could come from almost anywhere, such as on Dover breakwater and Llandudno pier, but generally you will find the winner on the end.

The method to use on a pier depends largely on the type of bottom you are fishing over. If it is flat and sandy then adopt the techniques for flat beach fishing and, if it is rocky, use rock edge techniques.

The one time when you may make a change in approach in a pier match is if there is a likelihood of conger being caught, when I would tend to fish with small hooks and baits on two snoods but with a big chunk of mackerel or herring on the other snood with a wire trace and 5/0 hook. Even if you do not get any congers you can very often take some beautiful eating crabs.

Depending on your financial position it is often worth having a few tickets to get near the end, if that is the kind of pier you are fishing on. Most sea fishing matches allow double drawing and I have even treble drawn to get where I wanted. To find out what are the best spots on the pier, look at it at low water and get a rough idea of what the bottom is going to be like in each section. That way you are not fishing blind when the match starts.

If you watch everyone cast in at the start of a pier match you will see that all the tackle lands in a narrow band between fifty to sixty yards out. Obviously if you cast into this band as well, you will have only an equal chance with everyone else of having the fish take your bait as it swims along. The obvious answer is long casting to clear yourself of all the other sets of tackle and for your bait to be the first that the fish will see. There is also the disturbance factor, underestimated by far too many anglers, of all that lead being hurled into the water simultaneously which would scare anyone away. If you can, put your bait out past all the rest and you should score.

The next problem is deciding which side of a pier to fish. By nature fish swim into the current rather than with it so fish into the run of the tide rather than against and the fish will meet your bait first as they swim against the current. But there is an exception to this rule when the sea is rough: the tide is usually running that bit harder and fiercer and if you cast into it and try to hold bottom the weight and the tackle will ride up off the bottom when the fish you are after are most likely bottom feeders. So in the case of a very strong tide or a gale, fish into the tide all the time to keep your tackle on the bottom.

Sea Walls

There are always a few contests every year fished on sea walls and they all depend on the type of bottom you are fishing on. If it is a sandy one then you might well be in for a lean time because these sort of matches are usually picked for the convenience of those anglers—and organisers—who do not like walking out on beaches.

If you are pegged out on a sea wall the best thing to do is to have a look round the wall before the tide reaches it and see what kind of ground you will be fishing over. If it just seems a barren expanse, with nothing but sand for miles, then your best bet is to try fishing right underneath the wall where there will be a flow of current which might persuade one or two flounders to congregate.

If, on the other hand, the wall you are pegged out on is rocky and weedy then fishing is an attractive proposition. You can always pick up a few codling on these stretches and, indeed, sea walls like this can often produce top weights. The decision on where to fish on sea walls is very much taken out of your hands as they are often pegged out to the exact number but if you have any choice in the matter then do try for a bottom with some rock and weed.

7

The Correct Approach

Match fishing is like any competitive sport in so much that you have to put a lot in to get a lot out. This is why the correct approach and attitude to match fishing is so important. Far too often sea anglers go to a match with the thought that they haven't a chance of winning against all those other anglers when, in fact, the main obstacle is their disbelief in their own ability.

Perhaps some sea anglers do have that little bit of luck with them that makes them win time and time again, but that is no reason why the rest of the field should not do well. The important thing is not just winning but doing well at every venue. If you can catch fish well and consistently wherever you go, then your time for the spotlights will come. You just have to keep on trying.

The correct approach in a more practical sense means arriving at the match with plenty of time to spare. Even if I know the beach and do not want to have a scout round before the start. I always aim on getting down to the headquarters two hours before the start.

This allows for any build-up in the registration queue and any sorting out you may have to do on the beach or where you are going to fish. If the match is a 'rover' or 'fish where you want but stay in the same place as your first cast', then quite obviously all the best spots are going to go very soon and in a case like that I would like to be at my selected spot hours in advance of the match starting time. That way I know I am in with a chance.

Why every angler does not enter every optional pool he can, never cease to amaze me. It must be this attitude of 'I don't stand a chance'. But if you had seen as many matches as I have where the winner has missed out on a big cash bonus because he was not in the pools, then you would never miss.

The strangest case of this I have ever seen was at Llandudno a couple of years ago where the optional pool was just 5p. For that you had a free trip to Chesil beach to fish in the British Championships. The free trip was won by a club mate of mine, and his position was fourth! The first three anglers had not bothered with the pool even though it was only 5p. The other time I saw a pool go to the fourth man was in a match where the optional pool was 50p—granted a bit more than what you would normally expect in a sea match—but chicken feed compared to the pools paid into by freshwater match anglers.

From the competitor's point of view, I would like to see three optional pools at every match. A 10p heaviest fish pool, which is something I do not like but a lot of other anglers do; a 20p heaviest bag pool and a 50p heaviest bag pool. The whole point of these pools is that they are optional and nobody is under any obligation to enter them. If you think that 50p is too much then you do not have to enter, but those anglers who do like the idea of a big money pool should not be denied the opportunity of having one.

How the pool money is split up is rather up to the organisers, but I do not like the idea of clubs taking a cut of the pool for 'administration purposes'. I would much rather pay extra on the entrance money and let all the pool money go back to the people who entered it, and I think most other anglers would, too. So on optional pools, the rule is enter every one.

Always keep a watchful eye on the weather when you set off to a match and if there is even the slightest hint of rain take along a mac and a hat. It might sound rather elementary to say that but in a match you need absolute concentration and you cannot do that if the rain is trickling down your neck and your boots are full to the brim.

Similarly, if it is cold make sure you will be warm enough and not too numb to reel in.

If you eat (and by that I mean an angler who must permanently nibble while he's fishing) then make sure that you have enough food and flasks to stop you from wandering.

At nearly every match I go to there seems to be a shortage of stewards and the organisers are always asking me to be one. I have a rule on this and I think it is a sound one. If the match is going to be one where there will be only a few fish caught and so that stewarding will not involve much work, then by all means help out the club by stewarding. But I will not steward if I think there is going to be a lot of fish caught and that I will lose some valuable fishing time by having to see to someone every few minutes. Similarly, I will not steward a match where the rules that the steward must go to the angler. You could end up by having to walk up and down all day with no time for your own fishing. It is only fair on the steward if he has to see the fish on the hook that the angler go to him.

On the point of stewarding, read your rules very carefully and see what they say about having a fish registered. If they say the steward must see the fish on the hook then do not take it off before he has seen it and expect him to mark it in on the grounds of your honesty. If he is a good steward he will not do it.

It is a good idea to get hold of a copy of the match rules before the day if it is the first time that you are entering a particular match. You can iron out anything that is not clear before you start, and many match rules are FAR from clear! In fact, as I write this chapter I have received rules from a match at Lowestoft I intend fishing in six weeks' time which gives me all the time I want to plan everything.

The common pitfalls in rule sheets are the size limits which can vary from contest to contest. I see that Lowestoft have a dab limit of 5.9 inches whereas some festivals are now imposing a nine inch limit on dabs. The whole point is that if you get the sizes wrong you could either end up being disqualified for bringing under-sized fish to the scales or, just as bad, find out that half the fish you threw back as undersize you could have kept. It is for this reason that a rule is essential in the tackle box.

On bait the approach must be positive. You must have everything you are liable to need and in quantity before you enter any big match. Allow for every eventuality and you will never come unstuck.

Venues that constantly produce low weights have a nasty habit of suddenly coming in with a super match weight because a shoal of fish suddenly moved in.

I hope, by this stage of the book, that I have convinced you of the need to learn crab fishing. It is hard to give figures of how much bait to take to a match because obviously it depends on the amount of fish you are going to catch, but for a normal five hour open where the expected quarry were flatties, bass or codling, I would take forty good crab or if they were small 'thumbnail' crabs, then up to fifty. This would allow me to fish comfortably with no other bait but crab for the whole match, if the conditions dictated it.

If there is any chance of dabs or plaice, then take along about sixty lug which again, if the dabs suddenly came on, would allow you to fish the full match with lug. If the beach you are fishing is noted as a ragworm beach then take along about a dozen 'super' rag—by that I mean king rag about two feet long—or thirty to forty small rag will let you fish rag if the fish decide to take it. This alternative bait is a sound idea for any match because, although I put a lot of faith in crab in summer, it can and does come unstuck sometimes; so in the best Boy Scout tradition, be prepared.

If this quantity of bait seems far too much for any match, then how about what I took to a recent match where the fishing was very fast? Ninety good crab, one hundred and eighty lug and forty rag. The reason I had such a variety and quantity of bait was that I just did not know what kind of fish I was going to catch. As it happened, I fished almost exclusively with crab and the other worm baits I gave away, but had the dabs been there as we thought they might have been, I would have been only too happy.

If the match is a small club match, then quite obviously there is not the need to go to all these elaborate lengths to have every kind cf bait in quantity and perhaps a good supply of crab and just a few worms will suffice.

Your tackle box is important. It should not look like a monofilament jungle with everything in a complete mess, so that you can never find anything and its contents blunt and rusty. Keep it tidy and well stocked so that should you need anything during the match—a spare hook or weight—you do not have to go on the scrounge for it.

Probably the hardest type of match to win is the one where you have to decide yourself where you are going to fish—the roving matches. It is fine if you live near the match and know just what is fishing well at any particular time, but for the away angler the task can be difficult.

What my team do when fishing these matches is to go the day before and split up so that each one of us is in a fancied spot. We fish to the same match times allowing for the tidal difference and at the end of the day we meet up again to compare catches. By doing this you can increase your chances tremendously but, of course, not every angler can do this. This is why I think it would be much fairer if all matches were drawn for places. Because a local knows the beach intimately or because I have the time to go to a match the day before is no reason why the bulk of the competitors who just go on the day and pick a spot should be handicapped.

In Conclusion . . . I hope I have succeeded in passing on some knowledge to sea anglers about the fastest growing branch of the sport. I claim no credit for much of what I have written has been passed on to me by anglers far better than me. All I have done is to bring together all the winning ways in one book. But do not become *obsessed* with winning. We are all good winners—what we need are a few good losers, too. The enjoyment in match fishing should come from the spirit of competition—not counting your winnings at the year end.

I won't wish you luck in your match fishing because overcoming the element of luck is the hardest battle of all, but I do wish you success. And if you are ever in the same match as me—I hope you come a glorious second!